APPETITES FOR

C000096848

Appetites for Thought
Philosophers and Food

Michel Onfray

REAKTION BOOKS

Published by Reaktion Books Ltd
33 Great Sutton Street
London EC1V ODX, UK

www.reaktionbooks.co.uk

First published as *Le Ventre des philosophes: Critique de la raison diététique* by Michel Onfray, © Editions Grasset et Fasquelles, 1989

English-language translation copyright © Reaktion Books 2015

Translated by Donald Barry and Stephen Muecke

Printed and bound in Great Britain
by Bell & Bain, Glasgow

A catalogue record for this book is available from the British Library
ISBN 978 1 78023 445 8

Contents

Introduction:
The Banquet of the Omnivores

I am much more interested in a question on which the 'salvation of humanity' depends far more than on any theologian's curio: the question of nutrition.

Nietzsche, *Ecce Homo*

Diogenes – farter, masturbator and cannibal – has invited to his banquet the most emblematic of dining companions: Rousseau, paranoid herbivore and champion of plebeian tastes; Kant, the austere hypochondriac, trying to bring together drunkenness and ethics; Nietzsche, the Germanophobe who champions Piedmontese cuisine in order to purify Prussian nutrition; the nebulous Fourier, who wants to be the Clausewitz of nutritive warfare; Sartre, the viscous thinker, comfortable with lobster à la mescaline; and Marinetti, the experimental gastrosopher, who combines the most unexpected flavours.[1]

From Cynical alimentary nihilism to futurist culinary revolution, many paths, winding and diverse, can be taken. They link men who are preoccupied – if we may venture the neologism – with *Dietet(h)ics,* understood as knowledge of tastes. On the banquet table of these guests we find raw octopus and human flesh, milk products and sugared prunes strangely transformed into sauerkraut, a rosary of sausages and a plate of 'Excited Pig', a sausage cooked in coffee flavoured with eau de cologne, small pastries, vol-au-vents and gutted crustaceans. Water for abstainers and wine for hedonists. Kant's Médoc and his choice of cod, spring water and clear fountains, Rousseau's curd and fresh fruit.

Those absent are otherwise occupied with their orders or their favourite foods. Descartes is too quiet. He, who in his Parisian period was a brawler and libertine, a hedonist and bandit, was not averse to taverns where a Poissy vintage, the table wine of the court, was served from the barrel. Or he would opt for a rough drop from the hills of Montmartre.[2] All we know about him is what the overly austere Baillet wanted us to know. It seems that more accurate biographies of the author of *The Discourse on Method* would be full of women, wine and duels. Spinoza, also, is silent. His life – as is so often the case – resembles his work: regular architecture, a machine without surprises, Apollonian in form. Colerus tells us that: 'He lived a whole day on a milk soup tempered with butter . . . and a pot of beer . . . another day he ate nothing but gruel served with raisins and butter.'[3] A few hours before dying, the Dutch sage ate some broth from an old rooster prepared by the people of the lodging house. Baruch's taste certainly seems plain. Based on the abstemiousness of the *Ethics* and the rigour of his proofs, one can hardly infer he ate like a new Gargantua.

Between courses Hegel appears with his wine from Bordeaux. In his hand he is holding a letter to the Ramann brothers that reads:

> I once more have the honour of requesting from your graces the delivery of a quarter *Eimer* [about 11 litres] of wine, this time Médoc. You should have received the money for the barrel: but I pray send me one that is in good condition; the last one was cracked on the top and some of the wine had leaked out.[4]

It is a pity that we have to deplore the absence of the essential – tears, laughter, wine, women, food and pleasure – in the beautiful artificial machinery that is the *oeuvre* of Hegel. We can only dream of a phenomenology of food . . .

A few paces behind him the niggardly Victor Cousin makes his way. He once confided that he understood Kant's *Critique of Pure Reason* the day when, in a German restaurant, a monumental plate was brought to the table, piled high with vegetables and garnishes, topped off with a ridiculously thin slice of meat: the basics reduced to very little. This corporal of the French philosophical ranks was a confirmed bachelor, a skinflint without peer and an inveterate scrounger, with nothing to recommend him except the passion for chocolate that was his undoing. This explains his need for thriftiness the day he invited Kant's translator, Barni, to lunch. After having ordered and eaten a copious meal, Cousin pretended he had an urgent assignment and made off, abandoning the bill to the forsaken translator.

Should we be surprised to read from the hand of Proudhon, militarist and misogynist to boot, a principled denunciation of Fourier's gastrophosy, transforming it into a vulgar 'philosophy of the gullet'? Is there any surprise in discovering that a Freud deaf, or rather *melophobic*, resistant to music, had installed a repetitive alimentary ritual in his house, providing the same casserole on his table every day, with only the sauces changed?[5] Resistance to gastronomy can teach us a lot about the genre, the work and the person. The denial of food and of the pleasure it brings is the parent of asceticism, whatever form it takes. It is also the cousin of renunciation, generating medical, vegetarian or vegan dietetics, those apparently rational regimens that are varieties of anorexia.

Others err through lack of conformity in their food. Thus the divine Marquis de Sade who, putting nourishment in the service of sexuality, elevates chicken breasts to the pinnacle, theorizing that they produce the most succulent stools for the greediest of coprophages.[6] Or Anne-Marie Schumann, who is only remembered by history because she was particularly fond of spiders, coyly preferring them fried.[7] Distantly related to this are Claude Lévi-Strauss's dining companions, who treated him royally with a bowl of nice white grubs, wriggly and crunchy on the tooth, but in the end releasing subtle flavours and delicate aromas.[8] Certain Gnostics have been just as much on the hunt for rare foodstuffs. On this question, we have to say a few words on the topic of *spermatophages* and their close companions the *foetophages*. Epiphanius, the Bishop of Pavis in the fifth century, relates that Gnostics wanting to take care of unwanted pregnancies retrieve the foetus with their fingers and, 'pound it in a kind of mortar, mix it with honey, pepper and various revolting condiments including perfumed oils'.[9] They took this meal together, eating with their fingers. Also distantly related are the Guayaki Indians visited by the ethnologist Pierre Clastres, who describes the pleasure they derived from sucking brushes soaked with the human fat that oozed from dead bodies they had roasting on the spit.[10]

We also have to mention those – neither lacking a sense of taste nor original – who (let us dream a little) might have been able to modify somewhat the rituals of 25 December, so that we no longer celebrate the birth of the Messiah in Bethlehem, but rather the feast itself: on a Christmas evening in Saint-Malo the philosopher Julien Offroy de La Mettrie was born. Known primarily as a doctor, author of a work on the treatment of venereal diseases, he is also the author of the admirable *Arts of Pleasure* in which he teaches the most radical kind of eudemonism. At the table, distinguished and sensual, voluptuous and delicate, philosophers with a taste for La Mettrie sacrifice themselves to the pure pursuit of pleasure. During the dinner,

> the bloated glutton, running out of room after the first course, looks like La Fontaine's swan, and soon has no more desire to eat. The voluptuary tastes all the dishes, but in small quantities; he paces himself, wanting to gain

most benefit . . . The others toast with champagne; he drinks it, in long draughts, like all voluptuaries.[11]

Later we find the rationalist gourmet philosopher at Lord Tyrconnel's table where a pâté is served. In his *Man-Machine* the thinker had already warned about meat that was undercooked.[12] But at the aristocrat's table, he fails to notice the advanced state of the pâté he is eating. Death is awaiting him.

Another gastrosophic Christmas evening: in the year 1837 one of the first chroniclers of gluttony, one of the fathers of gastronomic literature, Alexandre Balthasar Laurent Grimod de la Reynière, passed away. His grandfather, a pork butcher, had died of suffocation from a pâté de fois gras in 1754. His grandson displayed a striking eccentricity and was to be dignified by a similar fate. Born with deformed hands – half paws, half claws – he hid his palmate appendages under white gloves that also served to disguise a complicated metal apparatus that allowed him prehensibility. A devotee of the blackest humour, he sometimes put his hands on a burning hotplate and invited those present to do the same . . . He was also the instigator of twice-weekly, 'semi-nutritional' philosophical lunches. They were wry pastiches of masonic rituals, where one had to drink seventeen cups of coffee in the presence of sixteen dining companions; that is, seventeen people in total. The meal was theatricalized, the food the stuff of fantasy. Always the cynic, Grimod would test the faithfulness of his friends gastronomically by sending them notes announcing his death. He invited them to a meal in his memory. Thinking themselves liberated forever from an eccentric, the opportunists who were only lukewarm friends failed to show up. Others took the trouble. During the funeral dinner, Grimod appeared in flesh and blood, giving the lie to the news. Then, sitting at table, he carried on the revelry with the faithful. The only real faux pas he committed was to draft a pamphlet entitled *The Advantages of Good Living over Women*. But every eudaemonist worthy of the name knows that the two registers do not compete, but are complementary.

There are so many reasons to anoint 25 December as the celebration of feasts, the pretext for banquets. The establishment of other occasions would make up for the rarity of commemorations. Thus would the emblematic moments of philosophy begin to take shape: the melons that figure in Descartes' dreams, the apple that taught Fourier the theory of Attraction, or the omelette that was Condorcet's undoing . . .[13]

Dietetics is a serious modality of paganism, if not of atheism and of immanence. All transcendence is dismissed in favour of a will to self, serving as a gnomon of the real. There is a greater risk of alienation with any recourse to the outside or the beyond. In any case, it is not surprising that independently of his text and of the multiple interpretations given it, it is to Ludwig Feuerbach that we owe the celebrated, 'man is what he eats.' In his anonymous review of Max Stirner he writes: 'Follow the senses! Where the senses take over, religion and philosophy come to an end.'[14] And where life begins, one might add. Elsewhere, he states that 'the body is the foundation of reason, the site of logical necessity', and that 'the world of the senses is the foundation and condition of reason and intelligence'.[15] It is not irrelevant that Feuerbach was the first theorist of atheism, and the first genealogist of alienation. It was from his pen that definitive writings on the religious, on religion and its multiple forms, first appeared. The sacred is dissected, analysed and reduced, like a sauce. Feuerbach also developed a new sensualist positivity that derives more or less from a French materialist, then English sensualist, tradition. A modernity is taking shape that Nietzsche would soon inherit, and then pass on to our century. Food and sustenance became materialist principles for an art of living without God, and without gods.

There has not really been a science of the mouth as a pathway to an aesthetics of the self since Nietzsche urged us to take note of things close by, to make history from fragments of daily life. If we have to be cognizant of the approaches taken by Noëlle Chatelet, Jean-Paul Aron or Jean-François Revel, we also have to note just how silent contemporary thought is on the central idea.[16] Still, there is an exception: the late work of Michel Foucault, who became ill at the same time as an epistemological turn in his *oeuvre*. By the end of his *History of Sexuality*, the structures of the essential – love, pleasures, sexuality and the body – had been highlighted. After the appearances of the social machinery for excluding difference and producing normality, he moved on to the most secret but most exciting of mysteries. Finally a genuine Nietzschean concern for the essentials emerged.

In *The Use of Pleasure*, dietetics is described as something we might call an art without a museum. It is read as a way to 'stylize a freedom', a logic of the body at the same time as an apology for its mastery.[17] The choice of a food becomes what it really is: an existential choice through which one accedes to self-constitution. A genealogy of dietetics isolates medical care as a foundational principle: health is the aim of the dietician. The texts in the Hippocratic body of work should be read on this subject, and followed up with Galen. The evolution of this concern marks a progressive autonomy of mobility. The alimentary regime becomes

> a fundamental category through which human behavior could be conceptualized. It characterized the way in which one managed one's existence, and it enabled a set of rules to be affixed to conduct; it was a mode of prolematization of behavior that was indexed to a nature which had to be preserved and to which it was right to conform. Regimen was a whole way of living.[18]

A way of living one's life, certainly, but also a way of imagining one's body, fantasizing the future, making diet a part of future reality. There is no innocent dietetics. It advises us on the will to be and to become, on the archetypical categories of a life, a thought, a system or a work. Hence our interest in travelling this path among doctrines and books through the history of philosophy, to arrive at our ideas in an oblique and unfamiliar manner. Food is like Ariadne's thread, saving us from kicking our heels or getting lost in a labyrinth.

The art of eating is art *in fine*. Foucault writes: 'the practice of regimen as an art of living was . . . a whole manner of forming oneself as a subject who had the proper, necessary and sufficient concern for his body.'[19] With ethics merged with aesthetics, dietetics becomes a science of subjectivity. It shows that there can be a science of the particular as a stairway to the universal. Food as an argument that can penetrate the real. It is, in the end, a stratagem for the construction of the self as a coherent work of art. The singularity that it authorizes and the elaboration of the self that it permits have established as proverbial a Brillat-Savarin aphorism. In his *Physiology of Taste,* Charles Fourier's charming brother-in-law writes: 'Tell me what you eat, and I shall tell you who you are.'[20]

But let us leave theory there, because Schopenhauer and Rabelais are just fleeing the banquet where we had a quick glance inside. The first has just scratched something in the note-book where he regularly maintains a gastronomic commentary inspired by these banquets.[21] The second holds some recipes in his hand. One is about the aphrodisiac qualities of wine in which a red mullet has been drowned, and the other is on butter from Montpellier, which he noted on his Diploma of Medicine.

ONE

Diogenes; or, The Taste of Octopus

Hegel was wrong to write of Diogenes that 'we have only anecdotes to relate [about him]' and of the Cynics that 'they are worthy of no further consideration in philosophy.'[1] Quips and witticisms always signify more than appears on the surface. Cynical philosophy is possessed of a resolute will to say no, to flush out the conformism of customary behaviour. The Cynic is the emblematic figure of the authentic philosopher defined as 'the bad conscience of their age'.[2] Preferable to the obsessive idealism of Hegel is Nietzsche's fixation with the thinker as dynamite, 'a terrible explosive, endangering everything', through whose power he can attain to the Gay Science, the science of joy and jubilation.[3] Armed with the Nietzschean definition of Cynicism as 'the highest thing achievable on earth', we can calmly approach those regions traversed by Diogenes; through it we will find the impertinence needed for every new positivity.[4]

Our age of unyielding melancholy nevertheless bows before every possible illusion. The Cynical aesthetic of Diogenes is an antidote to this drift toward obscurantism; it is a will to lucidity. The demand of the Cynics is for everyday life to be shaped into an improvised but sober and pure form, purged of the dross and affectations of civilization. They want to sap confidence in the ideals that are the principles of illusion: the sacred, convention, custom, passivity. This demand is supported by a positive project of experimenting with a natural life as the condition of possibility of an aesthetics of the self, of a salutary pedagogy of despair. Diogenes, that 'Socrates gone mad', would no doubt have accepted the invitation of Montaigne – for whom 'our most great and glorious achievement is to live our life fittingly' – to create his own life.[5]

The Cynic is profoundly animated by the desire for an aesthetic resolution to the problem of existence. His drive is architectonic: better the enjoyment of a life under the sign of pure joy, of simple pleasure, than the despair of an everyday life of repetition, of the same. To an interlocutor who said to him that life is an evil, Diogenes replied: 'Not life itself, but living ill.'[6]

The philosopher in a barrel – although an amphora would be more appropriate, the barrel being a French invention – was to find a pedagogic use for food. The key to the theoretical edifice of the Cynics is the affirmation of the absolute superiority of the natural order over all others. Civilization is a helpmate of perversion: it filters out positive innocence and crystallizes the corruption of the real, transformed into a hideous object around which gravitate prohibitions, scandals and complexes. Artifice is to be banished. The project of Diogenes is 'the return to a state of nature' and nutrition is marked by this desire:

> In their theory and daily practice, the Cynics actually put into question not just the city, but society and civilization as well. Their protest is a generalized critique of the civilized state. It arose in the fourth century with the crisis of the city, and one of its major themes is the return to a savage state. In negative terms, it is the denigration of city life and the refusal of the material goods produced by civilization. In positive terms, it is an effort to rediscover the simple life of the first men who drank spring water and fed on acorns they gathered or plants they reaped.[7]

The Cynics' rebellion is directed against the norm, against tradition; commonplaces, whether of politics, morals or social rules, are swept away. Foodstuffs are a stake in this aesthetics of negation.

To the consensus of *the cooked*, which governs nutritive custom, Diogenes opposes an unbridled alimentary nihilism, distinguished above all by the rejection of fire, of Prometheus as the symbol of civilization. The first principle of the Cynical dialectic is *the raw*. The barbarization of the Cynics – the expression comes from Plutarch – uses omophagy as the basis of the deconstruction of the system of values on which civilization rests. Marcel Detienne asks:

> What, in fact, is omophagy, but a way of refusing the human condition as it is defined by the Promethean sacrifice and imposed by the rules of conduct prescribed by the use of the skewer and the cauldron. By eating raw meat . . . the aim is to act in the manner of beasts . . . in order to escape the politico-religious condition . . . via the low road, on the side of bestiality.[8]

Diogenes will go as far as the most sacrilegious transgressions: where others consume cooked meat, he wants blood; he wants his meat dripping. Detienne sees in this concern a commitment to 'the deconstruction of the dominant anthropology model'.[9] To refuse to eat cooked flesh, which means above all to reject the fire that cooking requires, is at the same time to oppose the civilization based on that fire.[10] The model for the Cynics is the beast, the animal. Time and again the anecdotes about Diogenes testify to his desire to learn from animals – dogs, obviously, but also horses, lions, mice, fish, birds and grazing animals. If we are to believe the stories passed down by Theophrastus, Diogenes opted for the ascetic life, the renunciation of the easy pleasures of civilization, after watching a mouse running about, transforming itself in his eyes into a model of wisdom.

In this mimicry, Diogenes will not be satisfied with his bloody flesh. Diogenes Laërtius writes that he even saw

> no impropriety . . . in touching human flesh, this, he said, being clear from the custom of some foreign nations. Moreover, according to right reason, as he put it, all elements are contained in all things and pervade everything: since not only is meat a constituent of bread, but bread of vegetables; and all other bodies also, by means of certain invisible passages and particles, find their way in and unite with all substances in the form of vapour.[11]

Thus a closeness to, even a kinship with animals is ensured, and not just any animals but the most cruel, the most savage carnivores, such as wolves, which, if we are to believe Plato, originate in allelophagy: 'anyone who has tasted even a single morsel of human entrails mixed in among those of other sacrificial offerings is bound to become a wolf.'[12] Nothing is more noxious than human fodder. In acting this way, Diogenes knows what he is doing – he ceases to be a man and bases himself on his animality. At the same time he introduces the seeds of an apocalypse in a civilization that does not tolerate cannibalism other than in its ritualized forms or as the only solution to a lack of food. Nowhere but in Diogenes is anthropophagy a considered act in the realm of the immanent. Tolerated, encouraged and supported when it is part of magical, religious or ritualized criminal eating, cannibalism is integrated into the multiplicity of social modalities, assuaging vengeance after tribal warfare, juridical sanction (Tartars concerned for the rights of Crusaders deceived by their wives while they were travelling to Jerusalem), a solution to get around the want of nutrition. But from the point of view of a social nihilist, it seems that the allelophagy of Diogenes is unique, without antecedent or descendant.

Diogenes' taste for blood does not exclude a practical vegetarianism. Diogenes Laërtius recounts the philosopher's experiment with human flesh. We do not know if he succeeded in
overcoming his repugnance in this regard, but even if it did take
place the experiment did not become a habit. It was rather a
'happening' in the Greek city. The anecdotes handed down about
Diogenes reveal him as a greater fan of olives and wild berries
than leg of human.

The Cynical eulogy on the simple life could be easily accom-
modated to the simple frugality of life under the Hellenic sun.
On numerous occasions Diogenes set himself up as a peaceable
gatherer of fruit and roots. He drank fresh spring water from
fountains, and the corners of his mouth glistened more often
with bright, clear water than with provocative haemoglobin.

According to Diogenes the provision of food is simple: nature
provides enough produce for us to be content with gathering.
He repudiates the kind of evolution that leads from improvisation to planning, from wandering to settling down, from the
nomadism of grazing to the sedentary life of breeding animals.
He places himself prior to civilization, before the choice of habitat
that restricts walking, the freedom of the journey. To gather
your food is to condemn yourself to the imagination, to submit
to chance and to refuse security. May I not, asks the Cynic, make
'the food of my choice the easiest procurable?'[13] You must limit
your needs to those of nature. Dio Chrysostom reports that
Diogenes

scorned those who would pass by a spring when thirsty
and move heaven and earth to find where they could buy
Chian or Lesbian wine; and he used to say that such per-
sons were far sillier than cattle, since these creatures never
pass by a spring or a clear brook when thirsty or, when
hungry, disdain the tenderest leaves or grass enough to
nourish them.[14]

In this way he practised a healthy life, a precondition for longevity.

A happy life on earth is possible through economizing on the useless and luxurious. The satisfaction of natural and necessary desires – the Epicurean imperative – paves the way for a naive joy, a pleasure in being. In fact, men are unhappy because they 'require honeyed cakes, unguents and the like'.[15] Frugality is another dietetic imperative. Water is the symbol of Diogenes' asceticism. Simplicity is the foundation of alimentary truth. He says:

> I get enough nourishment from apples, millet, barley and vetch seeds, which are the cheapest of the legumes, from acorns cooked in ashes and the fruit of cornel berries . . . food that provides enough nourishment for even the largest of beasts.[16]

In a letter to his disciple Monimus, Diogenes passes on the lessons that he learned from his master Antisthenes:

> the cups we drink from are not costly, but made from meagre clay. Let us take spring water for our drink, bread for our food, and salt or cress for seasoning. That was how I learned to eat and drink from my teacher Antisthenes, not that these aliments are to be despised – rather that they are better than the others and more likely to be found on the path to happiness.[17]

Several years of practising this asceticism, this philosophical life, led him to conclude that 'I ate and drank these aliments not as a form of exercise but for pleasure.'[18]

If the dietary practice of the Cynics implies a purification of the manner of eating and drinking, it also invites a simplifica-tion of the rites that govern them – neither organized feasts, nor specialized rooms reserved for that purpose of concentrating on activities of the mouth. Diogenes attacks the prejudice that says actions aimed at the satisfaction of a desire or the acquisition of a pleasure should take place behind closed doors. The Cynic initiates a politics of the displayed and exhibited body, as opposed to one that is hidden and shut away. Here again the desire for excess confirms the pedagogic character of Diogenes. Hence he did not hesitate to masturbate in public and to retort to those whose conscience he offended: 'I only wish it were as easy to relieve hunger by rubbing my empty stomach.'[19] He was no more averse to coupling in public, arguing that something so simple and natural could very well be performed before the whole world. Masturbation, copulation, why not nutrition? Totally shameless, he brought nutrition out of confined areas and placed it in the public space before the scandalized eyes of model citizens, who were accustomed to hiding away their meals as taboo rites.[20]

No life can attain beauty without a death that lives up to it. That of Diogenes is related to nourishment. There are several traditional versions of the way the philosopher took leave of the world. One claims that he finished with life by voluntarily holding his breath: in other words, mastery. Another states that he was the victim of a dog in a dispute over a raw octopus. According to the latter version he won the fight with the dog and succumbed to indigestion after consumption of his booty, in other words, punishment for the transgression of alimentary rules – unless it is a way of giving weight to the Cynical practices of the master. Plutarch reports the facts in this way:

> Diogenes ventured to eat a raw octopus in order to put an end to the inconvenience of preparing cooked food. In the midst of a large throng he veiled his head and, as he brought the flesh to his mouth, said, 'It is for you that I am risking my life.'[21]

Shortly before dying, he asked that after his passing he be thrown into the outdoors without a burial, where he would be prey to wild beasts, or that he be tipped in some ditch and covered with a little dirt.[22] The burial that would be given him by dogs, vultures, the sun and the rain seemed to him appropriate to complete a life of Cynical asceticism. When you consider how passionately Antigone fought to prevent her brother's body from being left 'for the carrion birds to defile and feast on' and how great was the horror of an unburied body, you can see the extent of the transgression that the philosopher desired.[23] In fact, in an ultimate reversal, Diogenes wished that in this way his body would be absorbed by some animal – a companion of fortune – so he could participate in the natural cycle, becoming merged with the elements. The eater of raw animals, Diogenes was to be eaten raw by animals. Animal among the animals. True to himself, then: even in death he continued to make food of all meat, and meat of all food. So there was no question of anything but this perpetual dialectic: eat, live/die, be eaten. Consumption, digestion, an infernal couple that proves the truth of the eternal return of things under the sign of the alimentary: nourishment as an argument for the eternal cycle.

In his diligence in merging ethics and aesthetics, in forging his existence into a work of art deriving from his pure will, Diogenes founded a logic of the use of the self where the mouth is the orifice of truth and meaning in spite of the silence demanded by every gastronomic operation. Taking nourishment rises to symbolic status and is integrated into the Cynical, nihilist enterprise. Lucian of Samosata had his Cynic say that his aspirations 'are . . . considerably different from other people's', and, further on, '[I] lead a quiet life, doing as I will and keeping the company I want.'[24] This is why we must not be surprised to see the philosopher enter the theatre via the exit, or walking backwards under the portico. He responds to those who object: 'This . . . is what I have been doing all my life.'[25]

Raw meat, the provocative taste of blood, the call to cannibalism, a frugal life, and meals taken publicly on the agora all testify to a powerful drive to nihilism – a negative moment supported by an ascetic will, a positive moment within the logic of Cynicism. From this point of view nourishment has the function of illustrating the claims of nature, of furnishing immanent arguments: it expresses the refusal of one world, that of artifice, at the same time as the desire for another, that of simplicity. Diogenes and his octopus show that there can be no innocent dietetics.

TWO

Rousseau; or, The Milky Way

If an emblematic figure were needed to represent gastronomic self-denial, the first person chosen would be Jean-Jacques Rousseau. In the same way, if the word *senseless* were to be used to mean 'devoid of senses and sensation', then that would be the word for the citizen of Geneva. He puts up with sustenance because it is the only way to stay alive; otherwise Rousseau would certainly turn up his nose at all food without much trouble.

We know about this philosopher's obsessive critique of modernity and his own times, and of his corresponding predilection for a natural humanity that is nothing less than mythical. His *Discourse on the Sciences and the Arts* would be a worthy addition to any collection of obscurantist writings, with its critique of commerce, of manners, of luxury, of intellectual activities, of philosophy and generally of anything to do with culture from near or far. The printing press, 'the art of perpetuating the extravagances of the human mind', falls victim to Rousseau's sharpest critique, and he denounces it for the 'awful disorders [it] has already caused in Europe'.[1]

Still in his stride, he attacks philosophy's 'vain simulacra erected by human pride', making it the key to the vault of a genealogy of decadence: 'To the extent that the taste for these foolish things spreads in a nation, it loses the taste for solid virtues.'[2] The figure of truth thrown up against the philosopher is that of the farmer or the worker.[3] Against the current of his times, Rousseau puts forward a model that is reactionary because it is inspired by the past, a rustic primitivity that comes before all-corrupting civilization. Virtue resides in simplicity, manual work, poverty and ignorance: 'the beautiful time, the time of virtue for each People was the time of its ignorance.'[4]

Agriculture versus culture. The idea will make headway. It is succinctly put; before long it will become a slogan. With Rousseau, a kind of *ressentiment* in thought takes shape. Progress in the arts is proportional to the decadence of the city. Eliminate the useless, bring about what is needed: Sparta versus Athens. To complete the portrait, Rousseau signs his name to the stupidest slogan ever: 'Man is naturally good,'[5] the necessary correlation to which is Nature as all that is fertile, rich and true.

Should we be surprised to read, in such a philosophy, a principled critique of gastronomy? Of course not. His whole *oeuvre* is proof of the author's fundamental powerlessness vis-à-vis any Gay Science, including the alimentary one. His justification of roots is worthy of the Spartan fanatic. Stew becomes the typical decadent dish. His taste for Spartan militarism is not clouded by the shadow of a doubt. Rusticity is the prime virtue of the bellicose.

The basic thesis that will spread so far and wide is that 'nature wanted to keep [us] from being harmed by science.'[6] This primal simplicity is the antithesis of a science of tastes, of a gastronomy. Rousseau develops a spartan theory – Nietzsche would call it socialist, or Christian – of food.

As a socialist gastrosopher, Jean-Jacques is so thoroughly imbued with populism that you might think you were reading the standard plebeian argument on the question of food. The luxury of the bourgeoisie and towns is the reason for the poverty of peasants and the countryside:

Gravy is necessary for our cooking; that is why so many sick people lack broth. We must have liquors on our table;

that is why the peasant drinks only water. We must powder
our wigs; that is why so many poor people have no bread.[7]

Luxury is the instrument of pauperization. Everyone in the
French Enlightenment, apart from Voltaire, was obsessed with
this idea.

The archetypal principle in the *Discourse on the Sciences
and the Arts* is that 'Everything beyond physical necessity is a
source of evil.'[8] This saying works for food as well as everything
else. Nietzsche would be overjoyed; here is a slogan of Judaeo-
Christian austerity being picked up by emerging socialism. Eating
is an imperative for survival, not for enjoyment. Commonplace
interpretations will soon have to deal with axioms like, 'One must
eat to live, not live to eat.' And watch out for the sin of gluttony!

Civilization has suppressed the natural in us, but it is not clear
how to find simplicity again, or how to know what is a natural
life or healthy food. In the hypothetical state of nature man fed
himself correctly because he trusted his intuition, which would
never deceive him. In this mythical time 'the productions of the
earth provided him with all the necessary support, instinct led
him to make use of it.'[9] Man's first task was self-preservation.

But evolution will occur. Rousseau points to changes in human
make-up, modifications to behaviour, new uses for limbs or
foods.[10] While Nature is certainly prolific and generous, she can
be difficult and inaccessible. Now, why would that be? 'The height
of trees, which prevented him from reaching their fruits, the
competition of animals that sought to eat these fruits', and various
other impediments force humans to adapt, which gives rise to
agility, strength and vigour.[11]

While he remains silent on what is driving evolution to lead
tragically and inexorably to civilization, Rousseau describes
the dialectical nature of the movement that leads to its development. The harshness of the seasons, the disparity of climates and
geographic and geological imperatives are spurs to initiative.

People living near rivers invent hooks and fishing and make themselves masters and owners of watercourses, lakes, ponds and seas. They

> became fishermen and icthyophagous. In forests they made for themselves bows and arrows, and they became hunters and warriors. Lightning, a volcano, or some happy accident acquainted them with fire ... they learned to preserve this element, then to reproduce it, and eventually to use it to prepare meats they had previously devoured raw.[12]

Remember that the raw belongs to nature and the cooked to civilization. In order to demonstrate his argument, Rousseau forgets this. There is no doubt that for the Swiss thinker evolution can be read in an alimentary fashion; from gathering to fishing and hunting, from the raw to the cooked, from berries to fish and meat – first raw, then cooked. As one way of eating succeeds another, modes of behaviour change along with them. An alimentary genealogy of the real.

Struck just as dumb about why a perfectly good and pristine Nature is condemned to evolve towards imperfection and evil, Rousseau sketches a hypothetical picture of the origin of civilization. Nomadism gives way to sedentary life, the family replaces solitary individuals. The group is born, and with it a new approach to food. Men become instrumental in hunting, women stay at home looking after children and doing the cooking. With this primitive division of labour, the male continues to be occasionally nomadic and the female is condemned to an absolutely sedentary life. Feelings evolve, language makes its appearance; rational organization and intersubjectivity have their embryonic beginnings. Inequality looms. A tragic turn is taken with the invention of metallurgy and agriculture. The first forged tools allow for the cultivation of 'vegetables or roots' around the dwellings.

The role of food in the Rousseauian economy of the real is not insignificant. Activities pertaining to food – that vital necessity – fall under a caste system involving the men who work the land. While the tool is made in one place, in another, with the help of the very same tool, someone is producing the wherewithal for survival. Some are in a position to produce more than enough. The desire for excess is the foundation of inequality. The wish for abundant food introduces the ferment of decomposition into history. The fear of nutritional lack is its negative principle. An economy based on scarcity would not have this kind of problem. The logic of lack leads to compensation through overproduction, which must be managed, from which arises property due to stockpiling.

Hunger is therefore the driving force of the real. It is hunger that leads animals to fight and tear each other apart. It is hunger that leads people to complicate a previously perfect existence. From wild fruits gathered straight from the hedgerows and ditches to vegetables produced in great numbers and stored, here is the whole trajectory that leads from wandering to putting down roots. The food of the wanderer is simple, healthy and natural and tends towards naivety, while that of the sedentary life is complicated, artificial and unhealthy and tends towards pointless elaboration. Rousseau never tires of opposing these two ways of thinking in his desire to revive the diet of our origins. This is the whole point of his bitter critique of gastronomy, his science of superfluity, uselessness and luxury, his argument about decadence and the perversion of taste. He will go as far as to write: 'it is only the French who don't know how to eat, since so special an art is required to make dishes edible for them.'[13] So what does knowing how to eat mean for Rousseau?

The answer is simple. Knowing how to eat is plain rustic consumption: only consume food that requires no – or at least the minimum of – preparation. To illustrate this proposition, Rousseau contrasts the meals of a financier and a peasant. Here is the menu of the man of the land: 'wholewheat bread . . . from wheat harvested by the peasant; his wine, black and coarse but refreshing and healthy, is the product of his own vine'.[14] Authenticity is signalled by the few transactions between the place of production of the food and the table where it is consumed. The only transaction that may be tolerated is that between the producer and the consumer. We do not know what the moneyed gentleman had for dinner, but at least we can imagine it when, one morning, Emile's tutor asks this question of his favourite pupil:

> Where shall we dine today? Next to that mountain of silver which covers three quarters of the table, and those beds of paper flowers which are served on mirrors with dessert? Amidst those women with great skirts who treat you like a puppet and insist that you have said what you do not know? Or, rather, in that village two leagues from here with those good people who receive us so joyfully and give us such good custard?[15]

Emile chooses excellence, 'all our delicate relishes do not please him . . . and he very much likes good fruits, good vegetables, good custard, and good people'.[16] We discover nothing about the menu, except that the cuisine of the wealthy is particularly notable for the trouble it requires in preparation and arrangement. It is worth far more for what it represents than what it is: the concern for refinement, for harmonious composition.

So while Voltaire invites his regular correspondents to visit him to sample 'a truffled Ferney turkey, tender as a squab and fat as the archbishop of Geneva', partridge pâté, trout with cream sauce and fine wine,[17] Rousseau sings the praises of dairy products, fruit and vegetables. As for the settings for meals, he leans to the rural, surrendering to the joys of the picnic. The ideal place for having a meal would be 'near a . . . spring, on the cool, green grass, beneath clumps of elder and hazel . . . we would have lawn for our table and chairs; the edges of the fountain will serve as our buffet table; and the dessert would hang from the trees'.[18] In a sense, Eden will be the elimination of the usual necessities for eating – tables, chairs and other utensils.

For Rousseau, there are no formalities when it comes to guests and staff: 'Each will be served by all.' He invites the passing peasant on his way to work with his hoe over his shoulder. Now the Garden of Eden is becoming communal. The philosopher does not exclude the possibility of being invited to local weddings: 'It would be known that I like joy and I would be invited.'[19] The pretty songs usually struck up on such occasions will brighten up the party.

Plebeian to the core, Rousseau writes in his *Confessions*: 'I do not know . . . any better fare than a country meal. If I am given milk, eggs, salad, cheese, brown bread, and table wine I am sufficiently entertained.'[20] And he goes into detail: 'My pears, my *giuncà*, my cheese, my sticks of bread, and my several glasses of a rough Monferrat wine that you could cut with a knife made me the happiest of gourmands.'[21]

As a well-informed dietician who wants to mould humanity to his image, partly by going through its stomach, Rousseau knows that a given type of food produces a given type of human. He expands on this idea in the *Julie; or, The New Heloïse*, where he says:

In general, I think one could often find some index of people's character in the choice of foods they prefer. The Italians who live largely on vegetables are effeminate and flaccid. You Englishmen, great meat eaters, have something harsh that smacks of barbarity in your inflexible virtues. The Swiss, naturally cold, peaceful and simple, but violent and extreme in anger, like both kinds of food, and drink milk and wine. The Frenchman, flexible and changeable, consumes all food and adapts to all characters.[22]

This idea – that man is what he eats – comes up again in the *Confessions* where Rousseau sees diversity in foodstuffs as the cause for human diversity. In his desire to control reality, the philosopher is thinking of developing 'an external code, which, varied according to circumstances, could put or keep the mind in the state most conducive to virtue'.[23] The domains he suggests as conducive for this project include climates, seasons, sounds, colours, darkness, light, the elements, noise, silence, movement, repose and, of course, food – what Nietzsche would call the casuistics of egoism – because 'they all act on our machines and consequently upon our souls'.[24]

So Rousseau is looking for a pedagogy of nutrition. The theory is located in *Emile* where he elaborates on this technique of nutrition as an invitation to a new, healthy sociality where the dross of decadent civilization is eliminated. Careful to theorize a pedagogy that his decision to put his five children into welfare would not have allowed him to practise, Rousseau begins by vaunting the merits of breastfeeding by the mother, or any other woman provided she is healthy. Milk is the perfect food. Do we need to go into its symbolism? I don't think so . . .

Nature sees to the needs of the infant, and 'in the females of any species nature changes the milk's consistency according to the age of the nursling'.[25] The wet-nurse's diet will be healthy. Peasant women are preferable, because they

eat less meat and more vegetables than do city women. This vegetable diet appears to be more beneficial than injurious to them and their children. When they have bourgeois nurslings, they are given boiled beef in the conviction that soup and meat both produce better chyle in them and result in more milk. I by no means share this sentiment, and I am supported by experience which teaches that children thus nursed are more subject to colic and worms than are others.[26]

To give weight to his argument, the author specifies that meat is subject to rotting, contrary to vegetable foods: 'Milk, although developed in the body of the animal, is a vegetable substance. Its analysis demonstrates it.'[27] The philosopher proffers a chemist's arguments. Milk from herbivorous females is full of qualities that outshine milk from carnivorous females. It is sweet, healthy and beneficial. In this apology for the milky way, Rousseau sings the praises of curdled milk. In support of this, he relies on travel stories reporting the existence of peoples who are entirely nourished on dairy foods. And finally, in the stomach, milk curdles and becomes solid. Rousseau is always on the lookout for proofs in science, and he writes that the rennet used for curdling comes from substances originating in the stomach muscle. The proof lies in milk being a food, and in addition being the simplest and most natural of foods. Rousseau will not find better; everything else is a substitute.

On his plate, the citizen of Geneva is particularly fond of dairy foods. He admits to 'a delicious snack' with the dairy products from the Jura: '*grus* and *céracée*, waffles and ginger-bread' as well as two plates of cream.[28] The philosopher comments: 'Milk products and sugar are one of the [female] sex's natural tastes, and as it were the symbol of innocence and sweetness that constitute its most endearing ornament.'[29] Else-where he writes that Julie is 'sensual and likes to eat, she likes neither meat, nor stews, nor salt, and has never tasted wine straight. Excellent vegetables, eggs, cream, fruit; those are her daily fare.'[30] Women, being closer to nature – and therefore the truth – have retained a healthier palate, one that is less corrupted by civilization. The advantages of a backhanded misogyny . . .

A healthy palate is a simple palate; men's versus women's. He is against strong and powerful flavours that are only enjoyed through force of habit. He is also against mixed or combined dishes. The miracle food and the emblem of the pure, the healthy and the true is milk. Everything else is corrupt: 'Our first food is milk. We get accustomed to strong flavours only by degrees; at first they are repugnant to us. Fruits, vegetables and herbs, and finally some meats grilled without seasoning and without salts constituted the feasts of the first men.'[31] Water and bread complete this healthy triad. The refusal of salt implies the refusal of the technology required for its production, therefore the refusal of civilization, which is in fact a Rousseauian obsession.

An unhealthy palate is a composed or refined one. And we can see that in the eyes of the philosopher composed means everything that is not used in its natural form. Wine, of course, and fermented liquors are among the products of civilization – fermentation, distillation, drying. Far too many processes for food. The use of alcohol is a civilized rather than a eudemonistic practice: 'We would all be [teetotallers] if we had not been given wine in our early years.'[32] No fermented drinks, and no meat either, because 'the taste of meat is not natural for man.'[33] The proof, for Rousseau, lies in children's indifference to a carnal diet, and their preference for 'vegetable foods, such as dairy products, pastry, fruit, etc.'[34] Concerned to preserve this tendency to vegetarianism, which Rousseau sees as natural in children, he writes: 'It is, above all, important not to denature this primitive taste and make children carnivorous. If this is not for their health, it is for their character.'[35] The ingestion of meat gives rise to cruelty: 'Great villains harden themselves to murder by drinking blood.'[36] Then follow, by way of proof, three pages cited from Plutarch where meat-eaters are likened, or compared, to dismemberers of corpses. It is an old argument, for which Pythagoras provides the model.

Still trusting in science, Rousseau looks for arguments for vegetarianism in the area of physiology. The way that our teeth, intestines and stomachs are put together proves the correspondence of the body to non-carnal food. Here Rousseau makes an elementary error of logic, specifically one of causality. If food produces the body and our very being, as the Genevan asserts several times, one can deduce that it is because it is vegetarian that a given animal has such a physiology, and not the inverse. Noting the same teeth and intestines in both frugivorous animals and humans, Rousseau concludes that we are related to herbivores – and pacifists to boot.

Rousseau's equation is a simple one: carnivorous warriors versus pacifist vegetarians. In his genealogy of civilization, he goes so far as to turn the passage from frugivore to flesh-eating into the passage from the state of nature to civilization:

> For since prey is almost the sole subject of fighting among carnivorous animals, and since frugivores live in continual peace with one another, if the human species was of this latter genus, it is clear that it would have had a much easier time subsisting in the state of nature and much less need and fewer occasions for leaving it.[37]

But why did the human species become culturally carnivorous, rather than remain naturally vegetarian, if Nature is such a source of perfection? Rousseau maintains an embarrassed silence on this point.

One more proof of Man's natural vegetarianism is that vegetable-eating species give birth less frequently than those that eat meat. Humans are among the longest to carry their young, thus proving their collusion with herbivores.

If, according to Rousseau's argument, natural actions are good because the dynamics of instinct must be trusted, how can the existence of people who eat raw flesh be explained? In his *Essay on the Origin of Languages*, Rousseau burdens the Eskimos with the phrase, 'the most savage of people'.[38] How can he come to terms with this savagery, and therefore its maximum proximity to nature, if it is characterized by omophagy? Diogenes is the only player who is an apologist for nature but does not commit the logical blunder. He justifies cannibalism and the consumption of raw flesh that are alimentary practices at the origins of our humanity.

In his critique of artifice, Rousseau does not include fire, that quintessential Promethean element, the very symbol of civilization. He accepts it, seeing in it a way of providing pleasure in seeing, in smelling, in heat for the body, and of bringing people together and driving away animals.[39] On the other hand he pillories the rationalization of agricultural production that allows for all fruit and all vegetables in all seasons as a major artifice. He opposes the natural run of things to the multiplication of greenhouses. To each season the foods that suit it. The desire to rebel against the natural movement of the year in a quasi-divine fashion creates irrationality, and failure in the quality of produce:

> If I could have cherries when it is freezing, and amber-colored melons in the heart of winter, what pleasure would I take in them when my palate needs neither moistening nor cooling? Would the heavy chestnut be very agreeable to me in the [sweltering] dog days of summer? Would I prefer it – straight from the oven – to currants, strawberries, and other refreshing fruits that the earth offers me without so much trouble?[40]

Rousseau's obsession is at work here: it evolves in complete fantasy from virginity, purity and irenicism. On the one side, perfection – naivety, innocence, initial freshness – along with its archetypal figure, the Peasant. On the other, the imperfect – sophistication, complication, combination – and its emblematic figure, the Bourgeois. Nature versus Civilization, Milk versus the Casserole.

Rousseau's theory of food is spartan: it is all about renunciation, asceticism and monastic rules. It carries the significance of self-disgust and contempt for the body – ready to be extended to the whole of humanity – shared by all the dieticians of absence and lack, more likely to be nursing their anorexia than concerned with any gastronomy understood as a Gay Science interested in lightness and enjoyment.

Should we be surprised to find in the gallery of famous vegetarians a few celebrated amateurs of blood and raw flesh? Two examples of celebrated herbivores: the first, Saint-Just, who was also obsessed by the Lacedaemonian connection. In his *Fragments Concerning Republican Institutions,* where, of course, he has his theory of liberty, a passage is devoted to the feeding of children. On the menu are bread, water and milk products.[41] The second famous vegetarian is Adolf Hitler. Need we say more?[42]

THREE

Kant; or, Ethical Alcoholism

In his thirties, Immanuel Kant would sometimes drink so much in the cafés he usually frequented with moderation that he could not find his way back to his home on the Magistergasse in Königsberg.[1] Every evening he played billiards and cards, and every midday he drank a glass of wine – never beer: he was the declared enemy of the Prussian national drink, 'a slow, but fatal poison' he saw as one of the major causes of mortality . . . and haemorrhoids.[2] To think of Kant as an aficionado of bars is somewhat surprising. The austere and rigorous pietist, the difficult and demanding philosopher was nonetheless a knowledgeable consumer of food and drink, to the extent that his friend the privy councillor von Hippel often joked with him: 'Do you think you will ever write a critique of cuisine?'[3] Alas, there was no *Critique of Gastronomic Reason*. Even when the thinker analyses taste, in the *Critique of Judgement*, he gives no place to food.

In his theory of the senses, Kant distinguishes the objective and superior senses – touch, sight and hearing – from the subjective and inferior – smell and taste.[4] The nose and the palate are organs of sensation without nobility, for 'the idea obtained from them is more a representation of enjoyment than cognition of the external object'.[5] The knowledge produced through smell and taste is not universal but particular, relative to a subject – hence its perceptual distortions. With the sense of taste, 'the organs of the *tongue*, the *throat* and the *palate* come into contact with the external object.'[6] Granted, but Kant overlooks the imagination, the memory and the understanding in the complex process of the production of a flavour and a judgement of oral taste. Without memory of flavours and combinations, without analytic and synthetic imagination, without both the global and particular grasp of the understanding, there could be no question of taste. And Kant knows it.

Smell is even less social than taste, Kant argues, for the latter 'has the advantage of promoting sociability in eating and drinking', and foreshadows flavours to come.[7] Kant speaks of 'the pleasurable feeling produced by ingestion'. But simultaneously smell has a solitary logic. To smell means to smell the same thing as everyone else at the same time, because 'others are forced to share the pleasure of it, whether they want to or not', and is therefore 'contrary to freedom', while taste permits a greater pleasure because it allows choice, selection, taking preferences into account: 'among many dishes or bottles a guest can choose one he likes, without others being forced to share the pleasure of it.'[8] Autonomy is preserved, sociability is increased, because in spite of its solitary logic, taste is the sense of sociability.

The exercise of taste is solitary and subjective: 'neither pleasure nor displeasure belongs to the cognitive faculty as regards objects; rather they are determinations of the subject, and so cannot be ascribed to external objects.'[9] Kant prefers the senses that permit a universalizable judgement, the condition of possibility for accession to the True, the Just or the Beautiful. Taste only authorizes judgements of value relative to the person tasting, a limitation that cannot satisfy the philosopher, who is concerned with a science of the universal and with little interest in theories of the particular for which there can be no possible science. Taste and smell could never be the objects of a critical theory, which is why Kant could not envision a Critique of Gastronomic Reason, contrary to the claims by his Soviet biographer Arsénij Goulyga.[10]

Kant's only possible critique of taste would apply to the superior sensations of touch, hearing and sight, which is why we have the analysis of the judgements of taste and their favoured objects in the third *Critique*. However, let us be clear about Kant's failings in relation to art: his pictorial references are meagre; his knowledge of painting limited; his recourse to literature virtually non-existent; and his relationship with music is on a par with that of the hard of hearing who love brass bands. Wasianski affirms that 'he preferred blaring military music over all other kinds.'[11] A concert in honour of Moses Mendelssohn had turned him off concerts and he claimed that music was not worth the time it took to learn it. The time you devote to practising an instrument is spent at the expense of more important things. Its ultimate failing in the eyes of the philosopher is that music is condemned to express only feelings, never ideas. Hence his definitive lack of interest. Let us be wary of deaf philosophers.

No critical theory of alimentary taste is possible. The subject is too imprecise for a science. You could retort to Kant that imprecision was also the fate of the other forms of taste and that it is not possible to perform an objective analysis of any perception whatsoever – whether visual, auditory, olfactory or gustatory, or of touch – and therefore including action. Just the same, that does not stop the philosopher from here and there offering his opinions on food and drink, not to forget the gusto with which he tucked into an unambiguous nutritive practice. Borowski recounts that 'when he enjoyed a dish he asked for the recipe. He didn't really like complicated cooking, but above all insisted on the meat being tender and the wine of good quality. He didn't like to eat quickly, nor to rise from the table immediately after the meal.'[12] Picture Kant, between pages of the *Critique of Pure Reason*, recopying recipes to give to his domestic, Lampe, who like all ex-soldiers – as he was – was a little naive, but obedient and careful to prepare in time the meal that Kant always ordered for the following day.

Having emerged from the state of inebriation in which we left him in the 1760s, Kant pulled himself together and probably drew on the experience to create a theory of drunkenness. In his *Anthropology from a Pragmatic Point of View*, drunkenness is defined as 'the unnatural condition of inability to order one's sense representations according to laws of experience, provided that the condition is the effect of an excessive consumption of drink'.[13] It is also 'a physical means to excite . . . the imagination', to strengthen it, or at least to elevate its feeling'.[14] The instruments of this divine alchemy are 'fermented beverages, wine or beer, or the spirits extracted from them, such as brandy; [all] these substances [being] contrary to nature or artificial'.[15] Kant concedes that these techniques to forget the self can allow one to escape a world that is too harsh – to 'forget the burden that seems to lie, originally, in life generally'.[16] The philosopher theorizes about the different effects of these beverages – taciturn drunkenness from brandy, stimulation from wine and nutrition from beer. Their ingestion 'serve[s] as social intoxication; but with the difference that drinking-bouts with beer make guests more dreamy and withdrawn, whereas at a wine-drinking party the guests are cheerful, boisterous, talkative, and witty'.[17] Describing the symptoms of inebriation he has observed – staggering and slurring his words – Kant condemns drunkenness in the name of one's duties to society and to oneself, with however this tempering codicil: 'But there is much to be said for qualifying the judgment of such a mistake, since the borderline of self-control can be so easily overlooked and overstepped, for the host desires that the guest leave fully satisfied . . . by this act of social activity'.[18] God knows it is easier to tolerate those sins that one might have committed oneself! *Te absolvo.*

Persisting with the analysis of this divine consolation, Kant associates drunkenness with the carefreeness it provokes: 'the drunken man no longer feels life's obstacles, with whose overcoming nature is incessantly connected'.[19] Intoxication also encourages speaking freely, the opening up of emotions, and the expansion of morality:

> It is the instrumental vehicle of a moral quality, namely frankness. Holding back one's thoughts is an oppressive state for a sincere heart, and merry drinkers do not readily tolerate a very temperate guest at their revel . . . Good-naturedness is presupposed by this permission that man has, for the sake of social pleasure, to go a bit beyond the borderline of sobriety for a short while.[20]

Drunkenness liberates another man in the drinker; it releases a second nature that has no relationship with the first.

Supposing Kant to be only slightly drunk, his observation of himself will give him enhanced insight, while his observations of others will furnish the rest of his data. The idea of Kant stumbling around the streets of Königsberg has a certain charm – it makes the postulates of pure practical reason seem all the more devoid of imperatives. To Kant the problem is not as trivial as it might seem, since he devotes further pages to investigating the logical structure of human intemperance. In Part 2 of the very serious *Metaphysics of Morals*, the Doctrine of Virtue, Kant includes a section called 'On Stupefying Oneself by Excessive Use of Food or Drink'. Here eating and drinking to excess are brought together – both are vices under the heading of a lack of respect for one's duty to oneself:

> Brutish excess in the use of food and drink is misuse of the means of nourishment which restricts or exhausts our capacity to use them intelligently. Drunkenness and gluttony are the vices that come under this heading. A man who is drunk is like a mere animal, not to be treated as a human being. When stuffed with food he is in a condition in which he is incapacitated, for a time, for actions

that would require him to use his powers with skill and deliberation.[21]

Kant likens alcohol to drugs and other substances that are obstacles to wisdom, dignity and self-mastery. Always magnanimous, he continues:

> They are seductive because, under their influence, people dream for a while that they are happy and free from care, and even imagine that they are strong; but dejection and weakness follow and, worst of all, they create a need to use the narcotics again and even to increase the amount.[22]

In this lies the advantage drunkenness has over knowledge . . . Its drawback is that it is insufficiently radical: you have to keep repeating it. Otherwise, if you are to believe Kant, the technique presents several advantages. Gluttony – 'greediness', in the translation of Alexis Philonenko – is worse than drunkenness, because 'it only lulls the senses into a passive condition and, unlike drunkenness, does not even arouse imagination to an active play of representations; so it approaches even more closely the enjoyment of cattle.'[23] In his following explanatory note, 'Casuistical Questions', Kant ponders whether wine and its powers of conviviality can at least be justified, if not eulogized. The means of intoxication that confine one in isolation and solitary pleasure are radically condemned. Alcohol has some advantages in that it eases social interaction and contributes to the harmonization of human relations. The austere pietist takes over from eudemonistic practice for the final word:

> Although a banquet is a formal invitation to excess in both food and drink, there is still something in it that aims at a moral end, beyond mere physical well-being: it brings a number of people together for a long time to converse

with one another. And yet the very number of guests (if
. . . it exceeds the number of the muses) allows only a little
conversation (with those sitting next to one); and so the
arrangement is at variance with that end, while the banquet
remains a temptation to something immoral, namely
intemperance.[24]

The distinction comes down to moderation, in permitting a use
that is not a misuse.

In practical terms Kant had resolved this problem – after
frequenting public bars for his midday meal for many years,
he had decided to stop patronizing them in order to avoid the
promiscuity of these encounters. After the decision to take his
meals at home, he strove to establish a precise protocol that
would ensure he never dined alone, a practice he judged to be
harmful from a dietetic point of view. An anecdote recounts how
Kant, having no one to lunch with, had sent his valet into the
street to invite the first passer-by to join him. He usually sent
an invitation to his friends on the morning of his proposed lunch,
so as not to deprive them of any other possible engagement.
The cook prepared the meals the philosopher had ordered the
previous evening. R. B. Jachmann writes: 'Kant was so attentive
to his guests that he took careful note of their preferences and
had those dishes prepared for them.'[25] His household was set
up for six people, and he practised Chesterton's principle: never
invite more than nine guests – the number of the Muses – but
usually only three or five. The meal would last until four or five
in the afternoon. As he got older, Kant discontinued the after-
lunch strolls he took to aid his digestion in favour of one or
two cups of coffee and the only pipe he allowed himself during
the day.

While he sometimes received students (at that time university
courses were given at the home of the teacher), his habitués were
a future minister of state, the Governor of Prussia, a general of

the infantry, a duke, a count, a President of the Chamber, a Privy Councillor, a bank director and a merchant. Master of ceremonies, Kant would lead the conversation, steering it away from commonplace topics as well as commentaries on his works.

The midday meal was his only one for the day. Before that he had only a cup or two of weak tea, at five in the morning. He always took this alone – the presence of a second valet after half a century of the company of the first so unsettled him that he could not swallow a drop of his tea. He could not allow himself coffee until very late, although he loved the smell, but during his last years he relied on it to give a boost to his failing energy.

Jachmann tells us:

His menus were simple: three dishes, cheese and butter. In summer he dined with the window open on his garden. He had a big appetite and he loved veal broth and barley and vermicelli soup. Roast meats were served at his table, but never game. Kant generally began his meal with fish, and added mustard to almost every dish. He loved butter as well as grated cheese, especially English cheese, although he claimed that it was artificially coloured. When there were a lot of guests he had cakes served. He adored fresh cod: 'I would eat a full plate of it, even on leaving the table.' Kant chewed meat for a long time in order to swallow only the juice. He spat out the remnants and tried to hide them under bread crusts in a corner of his plate. His teeth were very bad and gave him a lot of trouble. He drank a very light red wine, usually a Medoc, and placed a small bottle of it next to the place setting of every guest. Usually this would satisfy him, but occasionally he also drank white wine, when he found the red too acidic.[26]

Once the meal was finished, he loved to 'have a drink', to use the philosopher's own expression. He drank a half-glass of wine said to be 'digestive, from Hungary or the Rhine or, if he did not have those, *Bischof*' – sweetened red wine heated with orange peel.[27] Paper that he did not use for his philosophical manuscripts served as a reserve he used to cover his wine to keep it warm. Jachmann also says: 'He thought the pleasure of drinking was heightened when he swallowed air at the same time, so he drank with his mouth wide open.'[28] This was the ritual for a long time. Then Kant grew old. His health had never been good; throughout his life he suffered from stomach conditions. It must be said that his medication was appropriate: some bitter drops in the morning had dissuaded him from the effectiveness of that sort of pharmacopia, and were quickly replaced by 'a small glass of rum, which ended up giving him heartburn.'[29] Neither drops nor rum – at five in the morning, Kant abandoned his stomach to its natural hyperacidity for many years. His digestion was irregular. Such was the scrupulous fidelity of his biographers that we are even privy to the details of Kant's constipation. The Freudians would rejoice – the sphincter and its role in the development of Kantian ethics . . .

In fact Kant returns to scrutinize his constitution on numerous occasions in his work. One of his biographers tells us that 'perhaps never before had a man shown such an interest in his body and all that concerns it' than the philosopher of Königsberg.[30] In the chapter devoted to hypochondria in *The Conflict of the Faculties*, he confesses:

I myself have a natural disposition to hypochondria because of my flat and narrow chest, which leaves little room for the movement of the heart and lungs; and in the early years this disposition made me almost weary of life. But by reflecting that, if the cause of this oppression of the heart was purely mechanical, nothing could be done about it, I soon came to pay no attention to it.[31]

Kant is particularly concerned with what he calls a *dietetics*, defined as 'the art of preventing disease', as opposed to *therapeutics*, or the art of healing. A chapter of the work is entitled 'The Power of the Mind to Master its Morbid Feelings by Sheer Resolution'.

Hypochondria, which Kant himself admits to, is defined several times in his work. In the 'Essay on the Maladies of the Head', he writes:

> The hypochondriac has an ill which, regardless which place it may have as its main seat, nevertheless in all likelihood migrates incessantly through the nerve tissue to all parts of the body. It draws above all a melancholic haze around the seat of the soul such that the patient feels in himself the illusion of almost all maladies of which he as much as hears.[32]

He also says elsewhere on the topic, that he 'is not seldom weary of himself as well as of the world'.[33] In another text on mental illnesses he establishes that the digestive organs are the seat of these psychological disorders.[34] Kant's own predilection for the consolations and techniques of the aperitif for self-forgetting is understandable – the rigorous master of the categorical imperative is a pessimistic hypochondriac looking for an effective consolation.

Thus he develops a 'hygienic system' of which the postulate is: dominate your nature or it will dominate you. The principles are multiple and diverse: in relation to temperature, Kant suggests keeping the feet cool and the head warm; in relation to sleep, sleep little (the bed is a nest for a lot of illnesses); in relation to a propitious moment: think about it for a while (never at mealtimes), synchronize the activities of the stomach and the mind, breathe for a while – to 'suppress and prevent morbid accidents' – with the lips closed, and other picturesque details.

Where eating is concerned, trust in your appetite, have regular eating habits, avoid too much liquid – such as in soups – and as you grow older choose 'stronger flavoured food and more exciting drinks (for example wine)', in order adequately to stimulate 'the *vermicular* movement of the intestines' and the circulatory system.[35] Do not immediately give in to your desire to drink water. Have a single meal a day, at lunchtime, in order to reduce the amount of intestinal labour required: 'For this reason, an impulse to have an evening meal after an adequate and satisfying one at midday can be considered a pathological feeling; and one can master it so completely by a firm resolution that one gradually ceases to feel these attacks at all.'[36] In this way Kant illustrates the idea by which

> the *stoic* way of life (*sustine et abstine*) belongs, as the principle of [dietetics], to practical philosophy not only as the doctrine of virtue but also as the science of medicine. Medical science is philosophical when the sheer power of man's reason to master his sensuous feelings by a self-imposed principle determines his manner of living.[37]

Reconciled with philosophy, dietetics wins its spurs of nobility – it is understood as an argument for a science of bodily wisdom.

Emaciated, 'dried up like a clay pot',[38] complaining about the sauerkraut being too sweet while lunching on sweetened prunes, eating meat on the turn (because it is more tender), chewing it for a long time to extract the juice, giving up his fork for a small spoon, Kant burdened his correspondence with Kiesewetter about what beetroots to order. As an octogenarian reaping the benefits of a careful diet, Kant finished his life quite gently, comfortably. In 1798 he had written: 'The art of prolonging human life leads to this: that in the end one is tolerated among the living only because of the animal functions one performs – not a particularly amusing situation.'[39] True to himself, nourished on bread and butter (for which he developed an obsession during his last days), taste out of kilter, appetite gone, when he discovered food on his plate that had been badly and unevenly cut, he cried: 'Give me form, precise form . . .'[40]

FOUR

Fourier; or, The Pivotal Little Pie

The will to modify reality has rarely been more evident than in Charles Fourier, the astonishing poet of socialist utopia. His life's project was a striving towards the creation of a new world. His practice consisted of inventing an unprecedented style of living, with nothing left to chance. The new order along Fourierist lines requires grids, squares, situations, calculations and naming. With him the Cartesian project was realized – at least theoretically – in its most absolute and exuberant form, where one becomes master and proprietor of nature.

This philosopher – who they say never laughed – proposed a system that left no fragment of reality untouched. Climates would be revolutionized along with human morphology. For example, through the passage from the state of Civilization to that of Harmony the average height of the human race would be raised to 7 feet. Likewise, in his Combined Order, there would be an 'average life-span of 144 years'.[1] A rearrangement of the stars would lead to the creation of a third sex. The climate would be transformed – hot and cold inverted, the seasons improved, microclimates instituted. As for geography, Fourier envisaged a continental rearrangement that would take South America further north, and Africa further south, tectonic plates somehow obeying human designs. In similar fashion, cities would be changed. In this flurry of activity, the planets would be displaced. Towards the end of these periods of 'regeneration of our race',[2] people would see that they were now equipped with an *archibras*, or tail, a perfect and ornamental limb, the distinctive sign of the human labour force working efficiently. This appendage would grow from the body, would be sensitive like an elephant's trunk, and could work as a parachute. Fourier elaborates the qualities of this new limb as a 'powerful weapon' and a 'superb ornament', with 'gigantic power' and 'infinite dexterity'.[3]

Human relations will not be spared in this logic of novelty. Away with bourgeois couples, whose marriages end only in hypocrisy and adultery! Away with classical, exclusive, incomplete sexuality, organized according to the economic mode of production! Fourierist Harmony will reorganize sexual and other relations. In *The New Amorous World* Fourier sets out all his projects on the matter. In no particular order, he discourses on cuckolds – whom he classifies into 76 kinds (from the presumptive to the chronic, from the blind drunk to the laughing stock, from the careful to the clumsy) – condemns love in Civilization and urges the breaking of all prohibitions. The practices of incest and the orgy ('man's natural need') would be introduced in stages, to spare people's sensitivities.[4] Particular care would be taken to integrate all those excluded from sexuality back into the Combined Sexual Order: bisexuality, gerontophilia and paedophilia would become institutional practices.

In fact, Fourier's principle gets simpler the more its demonstrations get complicated. Desire must be liberated, drives given free rein, the imagination authorized to rule over the real. In a word, desires must be taken as realities. He writes:

Let us therefore study ways of developing rather than restricting the passions. Three thousand years have been stupidly lost with attempts at a repressive theory. It is time for an about-turn in social politics and to recognize that the creator of passions knew more about the subject than Plato or Cato; that God did a good job of everything that he did; if he believed our passions to be harmful and not subject to the general balance, he would not have created them, and human reason, instead of criticizing these invincible powers that we call passions, would have been wiser to study their laws in the synthesis of attraction.[5]

Fourier borrows this idea of attraction from the physics of Newton. For him it seems to explain the real as a 'divine impulse' to which humans are submitted.[6]

The new order sought by Fourier is Harmony – or the Social, or Combined Order – which he opposes to Civilization. On the way to Harmony from Civilization, the social world will pass through *garantisme* (public best interest) and socialism. These composite or ascending series will last 35,000 years and will culminate at a pivotal period of 8,000 years. Not even Genesis dared propose this teleological Eden, replete with qualities of pure perfection. In this economy of ideal becoming, gastronomy possesses its own particular power.

Fourier's idea is to 'organize general voracity', to manage gluttony as a passion that is shared by all ages, sexes and social categories.[7] It is dominant, writes Fourier in his *Theory of Universal Unity*: 'even with the philosopher who preaches the love of black broth, even with the prelate who denounces the pleasures of the table in the flesh'.[8] Beyond any improvisation or inadequacy, the theoretician of Harmony wants to envisage 'these pleasures according to the proprieties of the social state' and pushes rationalization to its limits.[9] Through the course of the writings the reader is thus witness to a strange alchemy which shows the extent to which reason, pushed to its extreme, leads to the irrational, along with its baggage of seductive effects crystallized in a poetics. Nothing is more bracing than this cavalier madness that juxtaposes numbers, words, ideas and images to the synthesizing ends of an alimentary regime.

This 'new hygienic wisdom' aims to elevate 'the appetite of the people to such a degree that they can consume the boundless quantity of foodstuffs which the new order is providing'. It is an 'art of increasing health and vigour'.[10] If Civilization is characterized by an economy of scarcity, lack and deficiency, Harmony, for its part, is rich with an economy of superfluity, excess and abundance. Penury is dismissed in favour of a production relevant to the needs of the Social Order.

Civilization's productive logic is wilfully blind. It deliberately ignores demand in its qualitative as well as its quantitative forms. Where the moderns cannot help but notice the yawning gap between the inappropriate offer and the unsatisfied demand, Harmonians will have only too much to choose from: 'surpluses will become a periodic scourge in the way shortages are today'.[11] Thus, 'to ensure the consumption of their surplus, they will need to get down to the details of individual predilections, differentiated according to temperament, a theory which will require the concurrence of four sciences: chemistry, agronomy, medicine and culinary science'.[12] The organization of this production will be done by a particular category of intellectual, the gastrosopher.

The gastrosopher is, first of all, an old man. He will be over 80 years old and will have on numerous occasions demonstrated his excellence in the domains covered by his discipline. An emeritus dietician, agriculturalist, doctor, sage and taster, it is he who decides on the subject of food on the occasion of the meetings conceived to this end.[13] 'The gastrosophers . . . become the unofficial doctors for each individual, preserving their health through the avenues of pleasure. They stake their self-esteem on the reputation for appetite and the vast consumption of each phalanx.'[14] These sages manage the surplus and develop the dietary regimen of the members of the phalanx according to eudemonic principles: food must be agreeable, light and capable of maintaining desire in its cyclical form. Their two aims are health and pleasure. They work towards judiciously adapting the dishes to the temperaments of the individuals.

At the other end of the age spectrum, children are busily playing, and for them Fourier has worked out a particularly thoughtful treatment. He knows their passion for food, and, from the first moments of their existence, wants a pedagogy of desire in place. In his vocabulary, it means finding a key around which to organize the children's cult. In order to do this, he interrogates the people in question:

> What is their dominant passion? Is it friendship? Glory? No, it is gluttony. If it seems weak among young girls, this is because Civilization has not provided them with dishes that suit their age and sex. Observe the inclinations of a hundred little boys. You will see that they all have a tendency to make a God of their stomach, and how many fathers, on this point, seek to emulate them? From now on, if Harmony is to establish a cult of gluttony for children, one may presume that fathers will enrol themselves willingly under the two banners, and they will link the cult of love to that of good eating, which will be the sole province of children.[15]

Gluttony becomes the axis around which the social world will turn. Against the civilized state and its abominable unripe fruit, Fourier will legitimize the sweet. If Civilization is characterized by lack, it is also characterized by acidity. In consequence, Harmony will be distinguished by abundance and the sweet. This explains Fourier's project of transforming the sea, when the social world reaches its culmination, into a huge expanse of lemonade. Harmonious truth is syrupy: 'jam, sweetened cream, lemonade etc. . . . will be the cheap food of children in the Combined Order.'[16] He explains the principle of this gastronomic innovation like this: 'Fruit with sugar must become the bread of Harmony, the staple of peoples who have become rich and happy.'[17] The cherubs will be brought up on a strict diet of preserves and jams, composite and harmonious mixtures of sugar and fruit, products from the two cultural zones of the globe.

The alimentary pedagogy directed towards children will be carried out in a systematic and reasoned way. From an early age, they will observe 'gastronomic debates on culinary preparation', then, in order to align theory with practice, they will eat. 'It will be sufficient', writes Fourier,

> to give the children free reign to attraction. First it will lead them to gourmandize, to cabalistic meetings on the subtlety of tastes. Then, once they are passionate about this, they will take part in cooking, and from the moment the cabalists have graduated and tired themselves out in consumption and preparation, they will extend themselves, the very next day, in labours of animal and vegetable production, labours where the child will cook strengthened by the knowledge and ambition that have bloomed at the table as much as in the kitchen. Thus are the natural functions meshed.[18]

In this way, the children will have gradually made contact with all the elements constituting the new science of gastrosophy.

With this method, 'a ten-year-old child in Harmony is a consummate gastronome, capable of giving lessons to the gastronomic oracles of Paris.'[19] Fourier dislikes those people in Civilization who make out to be knowledgeable in alimentary affairs. He rejects the pretensions of gastronomes from the capital, calling them 'little runts who never knew the first thing about the science they claim to be lecturing us about'.[20] In the Social Order there are no castes jealous of their artificially manufactured prerogatives. Cooking becomes democratized, along with gastronomic flavours. The aesthetic and knowledgeable creation of dishes becomes 'more or less everyone's science'.[21]

Gastronomy, taught from an early age, is also a major component of a generalized economy of the social for adults. It rises to the exalted rank of a pivotal science: 'In the regime of the phalanx, gourmandize is a source of wisdom, enlightenment and social accord.'[22] It is also 'the principal means of balancing the passions'.[23] Fourier's technique for ensuring the legitimate pretensions of gastronomy to govern the social is to place it under the authority of religion.

The path chosen by Fourier effectively to confirm the jubilant and appropriate use of food passes through a stage of 'the application of the religious system to the refinements of good food'.[24] Fourier extends the religious metaphor, introducing the notion of a gastrosophical orthodoxy, discoursing on the *major sanctity*. This last quality is recognized by way of a diploma. It distinguishes those who, on the occasion of a gastronomic meeting, have succeeded in demonstrating the suitability of an alliance between a dish and a temperament. In Fourierist language, the major saints have the task of 'rating the power of accommodation of each dish'.[25] Less prosaically, they analyse the ways of using eggs, sauces, their accompaniments and their possible preparation from the point of view of particular temperaments. In the same way, they submit mushrooms to their wisdom, or the union of strawberries and cream. Evidently having decided to clarify his statement with an example, Charles Fourier writes:

I shall not pause here to describe the debating methods followed by the council, nor the manner in which the debate was established between the candidate competitors who propose such and such an accommodation as adapted to such and such a temperament, with judgement based on what the majority have found to work, as for example when strawberries with cream are appropriate. There is a very simple way, which is to observe in each *Tourbillon* [phalanx] of the globe which rank in the passional and material hierarchy is held by he who best digests this strange mixture; he will be the temperamental pivot of strawberry and milk.[26]

Obviously . . .

The gastrosophic council thus allows certain dishes to qualify as orthodox. It is a great honour for the gastrosopher to be judged worthy of determining relevant associations. The distinctions are hierarchized. The saints fall within one of three categories: 'oracle saints, or theoreticians expert in judging the suitability of a dish which each temperament should consume at each phase or conjuncture'; 'creating (*conditeurs*) saints, or practising cooks skilled in making dishes in strict conformity with the canon of the council'; and 'erudite saints, who combine the characteristics of the others – expert advisors on both functions.'[27]

Any orthodoxy gives rise to factions or heresies. Normally dissenters are nipped in the bud by being spoken to and being confronted with the results. The testimony of an alimentary fact is sufficient 'proof of the pudding' for the gastrosophic suitability of a dish. Otherwise, in the name of the freedom that rules in Harmony, Fourier concedes that there may well be no harm if local heresies exist where atypical, geographically limited associations are practised, in perfect coexistence with gastronomic truths. It is alimentary ecumenicism.

The liberal practice of the councils does not exclude recourse to wars or battles. As a theoretician and strategist, Fourier knows that gastronomy is politics pursued by other means. The Fourierist polemic is reduced to food. Combat aims to determine 'nice tastes'.[28] The philosopher is especially obsessed by *mirlitons* [almond tartlets from Rouen], little pies, vol-au-vents and pumpkin. He particularly detests the last of these, as well as badly cooked bread in which the dough is full of water. In *The New Industrial and Social World* he writes:

If Parisians were not such gastronomic vandals we would have seen the great majority of them rise up against this crass commercialism, and demand proper baking; but they are made to believe that this is a good style of bread, the English variety which comes from England.[29]

Continuing this Anglophobia, he criticizes the fashion for eating 'half-raw meat, with forks bent in two and almost impossible to handle'. Similarly, he rails against the proscription of national aliments at lunch in preference to tea – a 'nasty concoction', a 'drug which the English had to get used to because they have neither good wine nor good fruit, except at enormous expense'.

Fourier is not happy. In Civilization, dishes are adopted through mimeticism, sacrificing oneself to fashion, and ideas of the time. The essential is forgotten: hygiene, pleasure and the moral efficacy of food. Trickery rules where judgement should be clearly deciding. And the philosopher continues his critique of the nutritional practices of his time. Having dispatched missiles against the English, he insults the Italians through their vermicelli – 'rancid paste' – whose fashionability he abhors. Finally, Parisians are the most to blame, for allowing decadence to come about. They adopt foreign dishes, fake their ingredients, overheat their meats 'through forcing the animal to race; the merchant wanting them to jump over a hurdle'.[30] Agriculturalists no longer know how to raise their animals or to produce healthy vegetables. The barbarism is such that 'a five-year-old brought up in Harmony would find fifty shocking mistakes at the dinner of a so-called Parisian gastronome.'[31] In the Social Order, this kind of error is impossible. Dishes are adopted through gastronomic approval or alimentary warfare.

Fourier provides details on these peculiar combats. The aim is to 'create perfection in even the least of the dishes in each of their variations'.[32] Afterwards, the combats allow for the promotion of a country and its election to the top ranks. There are, writes the philosopher, 'nations whose celebrity [is established] on a *soufflé* omelette or even a beaten one.'[33] Teams create their dishes and juries taste them to choose a winner. The struggle is over 'pies, assorted omelettes and sweetened creams.'[34] There is no shortage of detail. In the kitchens, it is flat out. They 'prepare only the masterpiece which will decide the celebrity of empires and upon which the utmost care must be concentrated.'[35]

Anticipating future detractors, Fourier defends his polemical principles: 'At first people will call these battles over the prize for sweetened creams or meat pastries puerile. We could reply that the debate will be no more ridiculous than our religious wars about transubstantiation and other quarrels of the same order.'[36] Thus emboldened, he goes into detail. War is one way to determine the excellence of an alimentary hygiene designed for the inhabitants of Harmony. Perfection that is capable of engendering, producing and maintaining perfection must be found.

The first confrontations take place with well-known dishes. No surprises there; the secret weapons are held over for the end. The definitive arguments earmarked to win the votes are kept for the final stages. The tasting begins. The battle rages. Taking the inventory of the troops and the kinds of firepower, the father of Harmony enumerates: 'A hundred thousand bottles of sparkling wine from the Tiger Coast, forty thousand fowl braised according to new methods, forty thousand *soufflé* omelettes, a hundred thousand punches mixed according to the councils of Siam and Philadelphia, etc.'[37] Elsewhere he introduces the sound of corks from 300,000 bottles popping at the same time, and tells us how many dishes are used for the cause.[38]

In fact, the outcome of the battle will be decided by pies, a secret weapon if ever there was one. One million, six hundred thousand have been made. Fourier reveals the reasons why he chose this particular dish:

I chose this dish because I was in the habit of reproaching the Civilized for their incapacity in this genre. I like them very much, but I have to avoid them because I am unable to digest them, which would not happen if our cooks knew how to compose them for different temperaments, and to add to certain types the flavours and vinegars conducive to all types of stomachs. In Harmony, the debate is conducted on this question. Its belligerent armies have to fight to see who will produce the best series of assorted little pies for a range of twelve temperaments as well as the pivot, so that each is provided with the kind he can easily digest.[39]

So the war came to its conclusion after the clash of the little pies. This is how Fourier narrates the surrender:

Everyone's spirits are so satisfied with the new systems and new little pies, the judicious choice of wines, and the excellence of the new dishes, that all the armies seem electrified by the delicateness of the fare. Even the oracles find it hard to disguise their secret approval and several among them, before getting back into their carriages, declare that they have digested the lunch and they would be ready to start again.[40]

Nothing is a better indicator of the excellence of outcome; the essential criterion of Fourierist alimentary hygiene is digestibility.

In Civilization, indigestion is the necessary conclusion of all meals. In Harmony, there are numerous courses because they are adapted to the different temperaments. Good fare is on the side of quality, not quantity, although the quality of lightness allows for quantitative abundance. 'The excellence of dishes and wines should have the aim of hastening digestion and accelerating, rather than delaying, the desire for the next meal.'[41] Faithful to his poetics of numbers – which delighted Raymond Queneau – Fourier divides the day into regular sequences to legislate on the gastronomic timetable.

Meals should not take longer than two hours. In each day, one can count five: morning tea [*antienne*], lunch, dinner, afternoon tea and supper. Each intermediate period is divided into three by two sessions: an interlude and a snack, which take no more than five minutes each. An hour and a half separate these two times. All stages are honoured with a good appetite. Fourier wants to maintain desire in an eternal return, and pleasures must be organized under this guiding principle. In order to illustrate this measured dietetics, this portion control, this erudite homeopathy, Fourier gives this example in *The New Amorous World*:

> What would we think of a loving spouse, an old friend, who said, 'I had such a good time with my wife last night that I am worn out, and I shall have to take a rest for at least a week.' We would all reply to him that he would have been better off managing it so that he could save some of the pleasure for the week he was going to be out of action.[42]

Wisdom comes from rational practice.

The right combination of dishes, and also of dining companions. Fourier considers a dinner successful if it is the occasion for joyous exchanges and pleasant encounters. He devotes a few lines to the 'judicious mix of companions, the art of mixing and matching people, to make them, through unexpected and delightful encounters, more interesting as the days go by'.[43] In order to avoid the boredom, listless discussion and inanities that occurred at the table before diners were matched up, Fourier brings into play the resources of the Combined Order. Successful meals are arranged for 'lovers, families, corporations, friends, strangers, etc.'[44] The philosopher even thinks, citing Sanctorious, whose pen he finds very apposite, that 'gentle coitus opens up the soul and aids in digestion' and consequently women should be invited to carry out their role as appetizers.[45]

All this contributes to preventative hygiene. With such medicines, who would dream of being ill? Only a few, most likely grumpy and unsusceptible to the pleasures of Harmony. The Fourierist pharmacopeia is not silent about them. As might be expected, it is food-related and alluring. Priority is given to the excipient. As opposed to Civilized medicine, Fourier aims to establish a new wisdom that would be 'the art of curing sicknesses with a little jam, fine liqueur and other treats, a spoonful of *eau-de-vie*',[46] in an infinite number of combinations. As treatment through taste, it depends on popular common sense that has always known to treat a cold with 'a bottle of hot and sweetened old wine, and a good sleep after'.[47] The link between treatments and pleasures is ensured through 'a theory of agreeable antidotes to be administered for each sickness'.[48] Thus he takes into consideration jams, grapes, rennet, apples and good wine as basic ingredients.

The excellence of these fruits is obvious if you know how to see the active elements in them as coming from the entrails of the cosmos. Fourier's dietetic astrology is one of the most astonishing parts of his whole work. In his *Theory of Universal Unity*, a chapter is devoted to 'sidereal modulation among temperate zone fruits'.[49] Having established that the state of society would allow for the modification of climates – and hence of production and productivity – through moving the planets around, Fourier expounds on a theory of astral copulation where (one must strive for the language of Fourier here) in a major octave, with a hyper-major keyboard, pears are created by Saturn and Proteus; red fruit are made, with a hypo-major keyboard, by Earth and Venus; in a minor octave with a hyper-minor keyboard, apricots and plums are engendered by the combination of

Herschel [Uranus] and 'Sapho'; while, on a hypo-minor keyboard, apples are produced by a Jupiter–Mars association. Various fruits flow from the Sun and peaches from the vestal star known as Mercury. Going into one detail, the author examines the genealogy of red fruit and puts his argument thus:

> Planets being androgynous and like plants copulating with themselves and with other planets; thus the Earth, through copulation with herself, by fusion of her typical aromas – masculine spreading from the north pole and feminine from the south pole – the cherry tree will be born, the fruit that subtends all the red fruit.[50]

Then follow the origins of blackcurrants, gooseberries, blackberries, raspberries and grapes, where we find, favoured with a question mark, cocoa.

Next, Fourier poeticizes foodstuffs, rather than presenting historical fact, combining his personal mythology with the occult, a peculiar rationality with a celestial mechanism of attraction. Each fruit is the object of a natural and symbolic history, as well as a futurist and rhetorical one. On this question of Fourier's poetics, Roland Barthes had a definitive formulation: 'replaced in the history of the sign, the Fourierist construction posits the rights of a baroque semantics, i.e.: open to the proliferation of the signifier, infinite and yet structured'.[51]

The blackberry is thus explained as the emblem of a pure and simple morality via a lyrical discourse on its brambles, its blackness, the alchemy of its colours, the logic of the tints, the Dionysian shoots. The raspberry is faded, so it becomes a symbol of false morality – a product of prickles, divided into capsules, the berry is the favourite haunt of worms. Then on to cherries, strawberries . . .

In this noise of the spheres, where it is appropriate to leave Charles Fourier, unfinished, in the company of a Pythagoras still resistant to beans, can be heard the faint echo of a soft autumnal song: that of the Utopian – or is it the stars? – lost among his mirrors, abandoning himself to the sweet delirium of food dedicated to Harmony. The old philosopher, who was also the brother-in-law of Brillat-Savarin, author of the *Physiology of Taste*, teaches us that poetic truth will not allow of demonstration. Its modality is the peremptory.

FIVE

Nietzsche; or, The Sausages of the Anti-Christ

The reader of *Ecce Homo* is asked to consider nutrition as one of the fine arts, or at least to give it the virtue of a poetics. The hyperborean science of nutrition is not unrelated to Fourier's gastrosophy – taste is given an architectonic task in an endeavour to resolve the problems of the real. Nietzsche calls 'the casuistry of selfishness' that care of the self that relates to nutrition, place, climate and recreation.[1] Similar considerations allow him to make a work of art of his life. The guiding idea of an active Gay Science lies in the injunction 'to be the poets of our lives – first of all in the smallest, most everyday matters'.[2] Dietetics is a moment in the construction of the self.

Nietzsche's concern with things that are close at hand, and only those things, assumes this polarization of the self. The reader is instructed in the hierarchy of problems as practised by the philosopher:

> I am much more interested in a question on which the 'salvation of humanity' depends far more than on any theologian's credo: the question of *nutrition*. For ordinary use, one may formulate it thus: how do *you*, among all people, have to eat to attain your maximum strength, of *virtù* in the renaissance style, of moraline-free virtue.[3]

The new Nietzschean evaluation makes dietetics an art of living, a philosophy of existence with practical effects: an alchemy of efficacy.

More than any other philosopher, Nietzsche has told of the determining role of the body in the development of a thought or of a work. He very early established the relationship between physiology and ideas: 'The unconscious disguise of physiological needs under the cloaks of the objective, ideal, purely spiritual goes to frightening lengths – and often I have asked myself whether, taking a large view, philosophy has not been merely an interpretation of the body and a *misunderstanding of the body*.'[4] Metaphysics as a residue of the flesh.

Nietzsche's purification of the body is somewhat reminiscent of Plotinian asceticism. For the loyal follower of Dionysus it is a matter of familiarizing the body with those elements that bring lightness, that invite one to dance. For a genealogy of the god of obscure forces, Apollo can be useful. The concern with dietetics is Apollonian: it is the art of the sculpture of the self, of creative power and of a controlled mastery. It is a subtle dialectic of restraint, of the contained and auxiliary energy of jubilation. Dionysism is a powerful alchemy: with it, man 'is no longer an artist, he has become a work of art'.[5] Dietetics is the metaphysics of the immanent – practical atheism. It also incarnates the principle of experimentation that founds the logic of the halcyon: the body is put to the service of a new aesthetic of knowledge. Nietzschean gastrosophy is a gateway to new continents.

In *The Gay Science*, Nietzsche asks thinkers occupied with moral questions – the 'philosophical labourers' – to reconsider their domains of investigation. He says that 'So far, all that has given colour to existence still lacks a history.'[6] Nothing on love, avarice, envy, the conscience, piety, cruelty. Nothing on the law and punishment, on the ways we divide up our days, or the logic of the timetable. Nothing on the experiences of communal living, of moral climates, or of the manners of creative people.

Nothing on dietetics either: 'What is known of the moral effects of different foods? Is there any philosophy of nutrition? (The constant revival of noisy agitation for and against vegetarianism proves that there is no such philosophy.)'[7]

A new history of this kind will inevitably bring valuable knowledge. Surprises will appear in the course of such investigations and without doubt diet is the cause of more forms of behaviour than people imagine. Thus, after deploring that 'neither our lower nor higher schools yet teach care of the body or dietary theory', Nietzsche establishes that a criminal is perhaps an individual who requires 'the prudence and goodwill of a physician' capable of integrating dietetic knowledge in the way he understands his cases.[8] Here we find a trace of Feuerbach, who says 'Man is what he eats.'

Diet determines behaviour, so could dietetics provide a way of transcending necessity? How can the non-existence of free will be reconciled with the possibility of acting on oneself, of constructing oneself, of willing oneself to be. To choose one's diet is to plan one's essence. Nietzsche argues that our choice is to accept necessity, which we must first discover. To illustrate his point he makes reference to Alvise Cornaro (1475–1566), the Venetian author of *Discourses on the Sober Life*, and to his work, 'in which he recommends his meagre diet as a recipe for a long and happy life – and a virtuous one too'. The Italian thinks the regimen he follows is the cause of his longevity. Wrong, writes Nietzsche: confusion of cause and effect, inversion of causality: 'the prerequisite of a long life, an extraordinarily slow metabolism, a small consumption, was the cause of his meagre diet. He was not free to eat much *or* little as he chose, his frugality was not an act of "free will": he became ill when he ate more'.[9]

In fact, you do not choose your dietary regimen; you only discover what is most in harmony with the needs of your own organism. Dietetics is the science of accepting the reign of necessity through the mediation of the intelligence – it is a matter of understanding what best suits the body rather than choosing at random, or following criteria uninformed by bodily necessity.

The concern with dietetics is a pragmatic illustration of the theory of *amor fati* as well as an invitation to the ascetics of 'become who you are'. The regimen is the will to self-harmony, the demand for the consonance of appetition and consent. It presumes the choice of what is imposed, the selection of the necessary. Hence Nietzsche's jubilation and his satisfaction at being 'so wise'.

How does one go about making a virtue of this necessity? First of all by determining the negative: what must not be done. Subsequently, the positive can be distinguished: what must be done. The negative dietetic is that of quantity; the positive, that of quality. 'To the devil with the meals people make nowadays – in hotels just as much as where the wealthy classes live!'[10] Overloading the table signifies the will to appearance: 'what, then, is the purpose of these meals? – *They are representative*! Representative of what, in the name of all the saints? – Of rank? – No, of money: we no longer possess rank!'[11] The meal as an external sign of wealth.

Nietzsche takes up arms against '*The nourishment of modern man* . . . [who] understands how to digest many things, indeed almost all – it is his kind of ambition.' Our epoch lies in the middle, between the lavish and the precious. In the meantime, '*homo pamphagus* is not the most refined of species'.[12] Vulgarity lies in the indiscriminate. The omnivore is a mistake.

A failure of quality, a lack of suppleness, of lightness and of finesse are the characteristics of a negative diet, of which German cuisine is the archetype. This cuisine *alla tedesca* is characterized by 'Soup *before* the meal . . . overcooked meats, vegetables cooked with fat and flour; the degeneration of pastries and puddings into paperweights!'[13] The lot is washed down with copious quantities of spirits and beer. Nietzsche detests the national drink, which he considers responsible for the heaviness of civilization.

He denounces 'that bland degeneration that beer produces in the spirit'.[14] No spirits either. In an autobiographical passage he confides that 'Strangely enough, in spite of this extreme vulnerability to *small*, highly diluted doses of alcohol, I become almost a sailor when it is a matter of *strong* doses'.[15] He experienced this as a high-school student. The right quantity is one glass – wine or beer – per meal. Bread is also to be banned: it 'neutralises the taste of other foods, expunges it, that is why it is a part of every more extended meal'.[16] Of the vegetables, carbohydrates are to be banished. Strangely, Nietzsche sees the excessive consumption of rice as leading to the use of opium and narcotics. In the same vein, he associates too much potato with the drinking of absinthe. In both cases the ingestion will produce 'ways of thinking and feeling that have narcotic effects'.[17] His reasons for this are obscure; no oral or symbolic tradition, no custom, provides support for these arguments.

Nor is vegetarianism a solution. If it was the choice of Wagner for a while – and subsequently of Hitler – it is not at all in keeping with Nietzsche's preferences. For him, a vegetarian is 'one who requires a [fortifying] diet', whose strength is exhausted by vegetables just as others are by what is bad for them.[18] However, out of friendship with Gersdorff, Nietzsche for a time experimented with a range of vegetables. In a letter to a friend, he opens up about his reservations on the question:

> The rule which experience in this field offers is this: intellectually productive and emotionally intense natures *must* have meat. The other mode of living should be reserved for bakers and bumpkins, who are nothing but digesting machines . . . To show you my well-meaning energy, I have kept to the same way of life till now and shall continue doing so until you yourself give me permission to live otherwise . . . I do agree that in restaurants one is made accustomed to 'overfeeding'; that is why I no longer like

to eat in them. Also it is clear that occasional abstention from meat, for dietetic reasons, is extremely useful. But why, to quote Goethe, make a 'religion' out of it? But then it is inevitably entailed in all such eccentricities, and anyone who is ripe for vegetarianism is generally also ripe for socialist 'stew'.[19]

Nietzsche's biographer C. P. Janz finds it hard to understand why Nietzsche associates vegetarianism with socialism, other than that at the time of his letter from Basel (September 1869) the city hosted Bakunin and the fourth congress of the International Workingmen's Association.[20] But that is not it at all. In fact, vegetarianism has its illustrious representative in Rousseau; Nietzsche is making his dietary regimen as close as possible to that of he who knows primitive man. Furthermore, the author of *Emile* issues a warning for carnivores: 'great eaters of meat are in general more cruel and ferocious than other men.'[21] Hence the equations meat = strength = cruelty, vegetables = weakness = kindness, which produce a division between the weak and the strong, and between aristocrats and elites, and democrats and socialists.

Nietzschean dietetics is a science of measure: neither excess (rice, potatoes) nor insufficiency (meat), and proscriptions (alcohol, stimulants) – in order to promote a harmony, a coherence between hygienic practice and necessity.

Housewives' ignorance of these basic rules of nutrition has produced a Germany that is coarse, heavy, without subtlety. Nietzsche criticizes 'stupidity in the kitchen', attacks 'the woman as cook' and inveighs against 'the dreadful thoughtlessness with which the nourishment of the family and the master of the house is provided for'. So 'it is through bad female cooks – through the complete absence of reason in the kitchen, that the evolution of man has been longest retarded and most harmed: even today things are hardly any better.'[22] For a long time the stupid idea has held sway that a man can be made to order at little cost – simplistic eugenicism or the mysterious management of the body. Nietzsche falls into the trap of this platitude and thinks that an appropriate diet has the capacity to produce a well-defined species, with distinct qualities. Nourishment as means of selection. A harmonious balance will produce a controlled vitality, for 'species which receive plentiful nourishment and an excess of care and protection soon tend very strongly to produce variations of their type and are rich in marvels and monstrosities.'[23] Plato falls into just as simplistic a mythology of dietetics as the instrument of eugenicism. Happily, Nietzsche does not pursue this argument. It seems that the hypothesis remains unique in his work and without further development. His lack of any major concern with collective solutions leads him to restrict his science of dietetics to uniquely individual ends.

To German cuisine, heavy and devoid of subtlety, Nietzsche opposes that of Piedmont, which he sees as light and delicate. Against alcohol he lauds the virtues of water and confides that he always carries a cup to drink from the many fountains that adorn Nice, Turin and Sils-Maria. Rather than coffee, he suggests drinking tea, but only in the morning, very strong and in small quantities: 'Tea is very unwholesome and sicklies one o'er the whole day if it is too weak by a single degree.'[24] He also likes chocolate and recommends drinking it for irritating climates unsuitable for drinking tea. He compares the respective merits of the Dutch Van Houten and the Swiss Sprüngli cocoas.[25]

Beyond the nature and quality of food and drink, Nietzsche integrates into dietetics styles of eating, conduct of meals, and the requirements of the nutritional operation. The first imperative is to 'know the size of one's stomach'.[26] The second is to eat a hearty meal rather than a light one. Digestion is easier when it has a full stomach to work on. Finally, the time spent at the table must be calculated – neither too long, to avoid putting on weight, nor too short, to avoid strain on the stomach muscle and excessive gastric secretion.

On the question of the alimentary regimen, Nietzsche confesses that his 'experiences in this matter are as bad as possible'. He continues: 'I am amazed how late I heard this question, how late I learned "reason" from these experiences. Only the complete worthlessness of our German education – its "idealism" – explains to me to some extent why at precisely this point I was backward to the point of holiness'.[27] In fact the whole of his correspondence with his mother testifies to the primitive character of his mode of nutrition, and this throughout his life. At no time did Nietzsche seem to want to break from charcuterie and fatty foods.

In 1877 his dietary programme was the following:

Midday: Soup, of a quarter of a teaspoon of Liebig extract, before the meal. Two ham sandwiches and an egg. Six to eight nuts with bread. Two apples. Two pieces of ginger. Two biscuits. Evening: an egg with bread. Five nuts. Sweetened milk with a crispbread or three biscuits.[28]

In June 1879 his diet is still the same, but he has added figs and increased his consumption of milk, probably to relieve stomach ache. There is virtually no meat – it is expensive. During the 1880s a large part of his correspondence with his mother consisted in orders for sausages and hams – of which he deplored the lack of skill in the salting – and in requests to stop sending parcels of pears. During the time he spent in Engadine he was concerned about his provisions and was constantly checking that he could buy tins of corned beef. In 1884 his letters told the whole story of his deteriorating body: stomach cramps, unbearable headaches, poor vision, vomiting. At that time he made do with a simple apple for lunch. Reading Foster's *Textbook of Physiology* converted him to the remedy of English beers – stout and pale ale. He forgot his anathemas against his compatriots' preferred drink, but it was to help him sleep – at least that is what he believed. The following year, in Nice, he lunched on millet bread and milk, then dined at the Pension de Genève, where 'everything is nicely roasted and without fat', in contrast with the Menton, where 'they cook like Württembergers'.[29]

Dairy products appear in 1886, in Sils-Maria. In a letter to his mother he extolled the virtues of 'quark with fermented milk added, in the Russian style'. He goes on: 'I have now found something that seems to be doing me good – I eat goat cheese, with milk . . . And then I ordered five pounds of malto-leguminose directly from the factory . . . Let's leave off the ham for the moment . . . also . . . the soup tablets.'[30] If the dairy products were for the benefit of his stomach, the consumption of malto-leguminose was not to facilitate digestion. As for charcuterie, it seems to have been dropped less from dietetic reasons than because the curing was dreadful and revolting. Lack of money, however, prohibited the hearty meals that he would have wished for. Poverty and physical deterioration create privation and reduce the latitude of choice. The lack of meat is what most upset him.

At Sils-Maria in August 1887 Nietzsche moved his summer quarters to the Albergo d'Italia and ate half an hour before everyone else to avoid the noise from the hundred-odd fellow lodgers, including many children. He told his mother of his refusal to

allow myself to be fed en masse. I therefore eat alone . . . every day a lovely rare steak with spinach and a large omelette with apple marmalade . . . In the evening some small slices of ham, two egg yolks and two bread rolls, and nothing else.[31]

At five in the morning he made himself a cup of Van Houten chocolate and then returned to bed to awake an hour later to drink a large cup of tea.

However, charcuterie was still a favourite topic in his corres-pondence – 'ham à la Dr Wiel', 'ham sausage' – as well as honey, chopped rhubarb and sponge cake. During his last year of lucidity – 1888 – he denied himself wine, beer, spirits and coffee. He drank only water and confessed to 'an extreme regularity in [his] mode of living and eating'.[32] But he still maintained the combinations steak/omelette, ham/egg yolks/bread. That summer he was sent 6 kilos of *Lachsschinken* (a mild ham) to last four months. When he received the package from his mother Nietzsche hung the sausages – 'delicate to the touch' – on a string suspended from his walls: imagine the philosopher drafting *The Anti-Christ* beneath a string of sausages . . .

Some weeks before his collapse Nietzsche finally began to eat fruit. In Turin, where he was staying, he confided that 'What flattered me most of all was that old costermonger women won't relax until they have found their sweetest grapes for me'.[33] It took until this period of his life for fruit and vegetables to appear in the diet of the philosopher. There was never any ques-tion of fish. In Nice, where fresh seafood could be guaranteed, he showed no interest in the produce of the sea.

However much he denies it, Nietzsche practises a *heavy* dietetics – a *meridional* heaviness certainly, a heaviness of the South, but a heaviness all the same. If German cuisine is undoubt-edly the densest and most indigestible, the Piedmontese cuisine he opposes to it is scarcely any lighter – apart from white truffles, the area's speciality, Piedmont produces stews and pasta, nothing very ethereal. There is no clear inflexion in Nietzsche's biog-raphy to show the influence of dietetics: 'Indeed, till I reached a very mature age I always ate badly, morally speaking, "imper-sonally", "selflessly", "altruistically" – for the benefit of cooks and other fellow Christians'.[34] In fact, with his ailing stomach, his deplorable physiology, his deteriorating body, his poverty, and his life as a nomad doomed to family lodgings better known for their cheap food than their gastronomic care, everything conspired against a beneficial diet. Where you might expect boiled or steamed fish (his mother had sent the equipment), Nietzsche consumed sausages, ham, tongue, game, venison . . .[35]

If you want to be Nietzschean, you have to remember what he wrote in the *Untimely Meditations*: 'I profit from a philosopher only insofar as he can be an example.'[36] By this standard Nietzsche would himself be discredited. He never puts into practice the dietetics of his theories. On the brink of madness he wrote in one of his books: 'I am one thing, what I write is another matter.'[37] Nietzsche's dietetics is in fact a virtue dreamed of, fantasized about, a way of warding off ingestion that all too often becomes indigestion. Food is an *analogon* of the world. Unsuccessful as a poetics, Nietzsche's rhetoric of nutrition remains an aesthetic of the harmonious relation between the real and the self, but once again an aesthetic only dreamed of. Dietary regimen also stems from a will to produce one's body, to wish for one's flesh. Faced with the pure necessity of disharmony, Nietzsche cannot save a will that yet had promised so much: the transparency of the organism, the fluidity of mechanisms, the lightness of the machine.

Nietzsche's dietetics is a fundamental driver of the confusion of ethics and aesthetics, one of the fine arts whose object is the style of the will. It acts as a support for the exuberant exercise of the will, or at least of the effort towards jubilation. Art of the self, banishment of necessity, technique of immanence, it functions as a theoretical logic and as a will to the ennobling of the body through a noble style of life. It is enough to give form to Dionysus while the stale smell of the Crucified still lingers. Gay Science . . .

SIX

Marinetti; or, The Excited Pig

Marinetti was obsessed by modernity in all its forms. He wanted Venice – a backward-looking city doomed to sentimentalism and decadence – destroyed. The Piazza San Marco would become the site of a vast car park. He wanted to make this jewel of a city, rising from the lagoon, into a huge industrial and military power capable of dominating the Adriatic and of assuring Italy's military supremacy, first in the Mediterranean, and then in the world.

The Futurists would leave no stone unturned to bring about their revolution. Urban planning, of course, but also music, clothing, cinema, novels – as many areas as Surrealism overlooked. Cooking was also integrated into the project of a transmutation of all former values.

With Marinetti, gastronomy becomes the instrument for the absolute will for change. He means to revolutionize the real through nourishment, to give it new forms inspired by Nietzschean lightness, by his passion for the ethereal. Marinettian cooking is the equivalent of Marx's organization of the proletariat into a revolutionary class. Through food it is possible to create the essence of a new life.

The rage of the Futurists is primarily directed at pasta, the symbol of Italy's past and the sworn enemy of its future. Marinetti writes:

> we Futurists therefore disdain the example and admonition of tradition in order to invent at any cost something

new which everyone considers crazy. While recognizing that badly or crudely nourished men have achieved great things in the past, we affirm this truth: men think, dream and act according to what they eat and drink.[1]

It has to be said that pasta, the emblematic Italian food, is the *analogon* of the peninsula. By attacking it, you can undermine the very edifice of the civilization. Macaroni, noodles and spaghetti signify Italy.

The ingestion of pasta produces a certain kind of body, 'a solid leaden block of blind and opaque density',[2] closer to iron, wood and steel than the materials Futurists consider noble: aluminium crystallizes the characteristics of weightlessness, light and speed.

For Marinetti the virtues are agility, the Nietzschean dance and a light foot. To achieve these, the gastronomic religion of pasta has to be abolished. It is a hindrance to spontaneity and produces ironic and sentimental sceptics:

> Pastasciutta . . . ties today's Italians with its tangled threads to Penelope's slow looms or somnolent old sailing ships in search of wind. Why let its massive heaviness interfere with the immense network of short [and] long waves which Italian genius has thrown across oceans and continents? Why let it block the path of those landscapes of colour form sound which circumnavigate the world thanks to radio and television? The defenders of pasta are shackled by its ball and chain like convicted lifers or carry its ruins in their stomachs like archaeologists. And remember too that the abolition of pasta will free Italy from expensive foreign grain and promote the Italian rice industry.[3]

Thus Marinetti brings together aesthetic virtue and economic concern. The demise of pasta frees the body from its submission to heaviness, and at the same time liberates the country from its subservience to foreign markets and presents the possibility of a national market economy. It thus allows the national production of rice to start flowing, and liberates the flesh from the shackles of gravity. In multiple senses the death of pasta signifies the renaissance of the body – the individual body and the political body. Dietetics as an economic principle.

The Futurist alimentary revolution will take nutritional virtues and needs into account. The economy will organize ways of eating and drinking in the interests of rationalization. Marinetti came up with this requirement during a meal served at the Penna d'Oca restaurant in Milan. His speech expresses the two temporalities separated by the Copernican transformation with which he is operating – before, pasta/after, rice; before, repetition/after, imagination. The frozen Italy of the past versus the mobile Italy of the future. Thus:

> I hereby announce the imminent launch of Futurist cooking to renew totally the Italian way of eating and fit it as quickly as possible to producing the new heroic and dynamic strengths required of race. Futurist cooking will be free of the old obsession with volume and weight and will have as one of its principles the abolition of pastascuitta. Pastascuitta, however agreeable to the palate, is a passéist food because it makes people heavy, brutish, deludes them into thinking it is nutritious, makes them sceptical, slow, pessimistic. Besides which patriotically it is preferable to substitute rice.[4]

Followed by a '*consumato*' of roses and sunshine', 'Mediterranean favourite zig, zug, zag', some 'well-tempered little artichoke wheels', a 'spun sugar rain' but also – showing it is not so easy to bid farewell to heaviness – a 'foie grasse', a 'roast lamb in lion sauce', some 'blood of Bacchus' and 'exhilarating Cinzano foam'.[5]

This Milanese declaration is valuable, above all, for the reversal that Marinetti introduces into the ordering of criteria for taste. The decision about what is good is no longer coming from the individual, with subjective judgements based on pleasure. The good is a national decision that takes group interests, the Whole, into account. Here Marinetti is closer to Hegel than to Nietzsche. The new system of Futurist evaluation makes the universal the gnomon of the particular. Marinetti effectively produces a critique of the faculty of individual judgement in order to promote the principle of judgement concerned with the common good.

Marinetti himself drafted all the Futurist manifestos on the subject of cooking. He coined the new phrases and established the revolutionary relevance of the key formulaic recipes in Marinettian language. The watchword of Futurist gastronomy is novelty. It is about allowing a new kind of celebration of food.

In the foundation text signed by Marinetti and Fillìa, the project is described is this way:

> The Futurist culinary revolution . . . has the lofty, noble and universally expedient aim of changing rapidly the eating habits of our race, strengthening it, dynamizing it, and spiritualizing it with brand-new food combinations in which experiment, intelligence and imagination will economically take the place of quantity, banality, repetition and expense. This Futurist cooking of ours, tuned to high speeds like the motor of the hydroplane, will seem to some trembling traditionalists both mad and dangerous: but its ultimate aim is to create a harmony between man's palate and his life today and tomorrow.[6]

They go on to situate the experience in the history of food:

> Apart from celebrated and legendary exceptions, until now men have fed themselves like ants, rats, cats or oxen. Now

with the Futurists the first human way of eating is born. We mean the art of self-nourishment. Like all the arts, it eschews plagiarism and demands creative originality.[7]

Marinetti's focus is optimistic, and he is quite clear about it. He hopes to modify reality through changing diets. Revolution through food.

Protest movements arose against this determination to turn food into the helpmate of change. One group of women from Aquila, on a campaign to save pasta, circulated a petition that was addressed to Marinetti. In Naples people went on street marches to support the persecuted foodstuff. In Turin a gathering of cooks took place where they debated the respective merits of tagliatelle and salami cooked with eau de cologne. Journals published photographic montages showing this pope of Futurism wolfing down a huge plate of spaghetti, while in Bologna a student, cleverly disguised as Marinetti, was discovered in the process of eating pasta in public. Some blows were struck for the cause by activist operettas and other didactic fripperies.

The Futurist revolution was carried out by quantity as much as by quality. So Marinetti favoured equally 'the abolition of volume and weight in the conception and evaluation of food, the abolition of traditional mixtures in favour of experimentation with new, apparently absurd mixtures . . . the abolition of everyday mediocrity from the pleasure of the palate'.[8] To this end, the new gastronomer invited the state to play an active role in the free distribution of a pharmacological alternative, where capsules, pills or powders would ensure the necessary balanced diet. A pharmacopoeia would ensure the proper allowances of albumin, fats and vitamins. The economy would be vastly modified by this: a reduction in the cost of living and salaries, and a consequent reduction in the number of hours in the working week. Here we find Marinetti espousing the ideals of all revolutionary utopians:

Soon machines will constitute an obedient proletariat of iron steel aluminium at the service of men who are almost totally relieved of manual work. With work reduced to two or three hours, the other hours can be perfected and ennobled through study, the arts, and the anticipation of perfect meals.[9]

Marinetti achieves the complete man that Marx was looking for. While the German thinker liberates alienated man through social revolution, the Italian thinker does it through a revolution in food.

The finality of Futurism is political; its teleology is aesthetic. Cooking is one of the fine arts through which one may come to resolve the problem of existence. Marinetti picks up on one of the young Nietzsche's pet ideas, that of the philosopher-artist: 'art represents the highest task and the truly metaphysical activity of this life'.[10] And since the philosopher-artist's truths include invention, experimentation, destruction, legislation and mastery, one has the right to make of Marinetti a new style of man for whom art is a way of achieving the transfiguration of the real. Undoubtedly Nietzsche would not have disavowed this manner of using food for apocalyptic ends.

The Italian people, nourished in this new way, would become virile and be able to impose their imperialist designs on the whole world – pasta acts as a counter-revolutionary element, getting in the way of the global expansion of a new Roman empire.

At the same time, the state's management of nutritional requirements frees the body of alimentary necessities, while it offers the possibility of an elitist and aristocratic culinary aesthetic. A full stomach responds to primary necessities. An aesthetic stomach allows for an artistic resolution of corporal necessity. The dilemma of quantity – for the people – and of quality – for the elites – opens up the possibility of a provisioning shackled to the Nietzschean concern to rethink humanity in the double perspective of masters and slaves. The popular eater is basically distinct from the aristocratic eater. The first nourishes himself to extinguish a primary desire. In his case, Futurists want him appeased in the cheapest possible way, with the help of the state. The second eats to consume works of art and to take part in the aesthetic logic of the revolutionary process. He ingests beauty. In both cases the end is identical: the production of a beautiful, strong, well-balanced, muscled, animalistic and mechanical body, one that is likely to respond effectively to the needs of the nation.

And yet, Marinetti's aristocratic rhetoric is pitched as broadly as possible. The master's utopia aims to aristocratize the masses, the crowd, to transform the people into an elite. The Futurist project is a sort of xenophobic national aestheticism destined to make Italy the master of Europe, then the world. Cooking is one way among others to begin to extract the people from abject mediocrity. Once the masses have become works of art in themselves, they will export their brilliance across borders. Gastronomy is the propaedeutic to planetary revolution.

Marinetti wanted to ensure that '*Every person has the sensation of eating* not just good food but also *works of art*.'[11] In order to do this, he codified the alimentary ritual. According to him, a meal needs to have the different elements of a table setting in harmony: glassware, china, decoration, place settings; the savour and colour of the dishes, along with their form and the reasons for their sequence. All senses will be called upon to play an active role. The art of combination had the function of preparing and arousing the desire to ingest. Sight is privileged; Futurist culinary art prioritizes playing with the pleasure of seeing. In order to intensify the visual impact of foods, the diners are subjected to organized displays of dishes that are destined, or not, to be eaten. The important thing is to provoke desire. Particular care is taken with colours and harmonies.

Touch, while generally neglected, is intensified by a peculiar scenario. First, Marinetti abolishes the use of knives and forks.

Fingers and hands are the new instruments for a pleasure he introduces. Touch appreciates temperature, distinguishes hot and cold, determines consistency (hard, soft, tender), knows the qualities of portions, grains, joints and smoothness. Small plates are invented that are encased in different kinds of tissues, or materials designed to stimulate touch – linen, silk, wool, satin, sandpaper. Particular tactile sensations are associated with particular foods.

Apart from sight and touch, smell must also be stimulated with, of course, the natural aromas of the dishes, but also with the concurrence of exterior perfumes that are likely to enhance degustation, which remains the underlying principle. So during the meal combinations of essences will be released. They will be carefully chosen so as to harmonize with the colours, forms and qualities of the dishes on display.

Hearing is sharpened in the same way. Music is transmitted through invisible emanations. Therefore, in order not to interfere with the senses, it will primarily be played between courses. In this way the palate and the tongue will avoid over-complex synaesthesic perils. To block useless noise, Marinetti proscribes garrulousness, chatter and politics at table. All effort must be concentrated on the sensations. Intellectualism and its complex turns of phrase have no purchase on such occasions. Poetry, as a science of rhythm, could do the same job as music. Think of the *lectio* in monastic refectories . . .

Finally, taste will be stimulated by

The creation of simultaneous and changing canapés which contain ten, twenty flavours to be tasted in a few seconds. In Futurist cooking these canapés have by analogy the same amplifying function that images have in literature. A given taste of something can sum up an entire area of life, the history of an amorous passion or an entire voyage to the Far East.[12]

As might be expected, Marinetti's theory incorporates the scientific advances of the day. So kitchens must open their doors to modern equipment: ionizers to give an ozone aroma to liquid and solid food – since ozone is the symbol of the wide open spaces of air travel for which Marinetti had a particular fetish; ultraviolet lamps which would activate and enrich foods exposed to their rays – thus multiplying their nutritive qualities (always with an eye to cutting costs); electrolysers that would isolate the essential properties of foods and permit the synthesis of essences – which, combined, would give new substance to revolutionary tastes; colloid mills, an example of modern industrial reason finding its way into the kitchen – these machines will facilitate the pulverization of flours, powders, spices and dried fruits. He will have to add to these new technologies, now domesticated for kitchen use, vacuum or normal pressure distillers, centrifugal autoclaves, dialysis machines and chemical indicators to precisely determine acidity and alkalinity in alimentary compositions.

All this theory was published on 28 September 1930 in the *Gazetto del Popolo* in Turin. Here Marinetti summarizes the basics of his programme and its mode of realization. Two categorical imperatives clearly become evident: the five senses must be simultaneously aroused for pleasurable ingestion, and the integration of modern technologies in the gastronomic process – the project being to construct dishes in the way works of art are created.

A number of banquets saw these Futurist principles come to fruition. As early as 1910, in Trieste, the first Futurist soirée was the occasion to reverse the order of the dishes. The first actual meal was contemporary with the theories and manifestos. The plates were named in a poetic fashion. Roland Barthes has brought to light the existence of a singular language, an inventive rhetoric, among those who discover new worlds. Marinetti is no exception. The novelty of the alimentary form calls for novelty in the language signifying it.

Thus with 'The Excited Pig', which is the name given to 'a whole salami, skinned . . . served upright in a dish containing some very hot black coffee mixed with a good deal of eau de cologne'.[13] Similarly, *aerofood* characterizes a sensitive combinatory art where the diner is served:

> from the right with a plate containing some black olives, fennel hearts and kumquats. From the left he is served with a rectangle made of sandpaper, silk and velvet. The foods must be carried directly to the mouth with the right hand while the left lightly and repeatedly strokes the tactile rectangle. In the meantime the waiters spray the napes of the diners' necks with a *conprofumo* of carnations while from the kitchen comes contemporaneously a violent *conrumore* of an aeroplane motor and some *dismusica* by Bach.[14]

This arrangement concentrates the Futurist commands: enhancement of the senses, elimination of place settings, use of auxiliary elements – perfumes, music, tactile rectangles – to make up for the asthenia of the senses for which civilization is responsible; the cult of modern noise, of the motor, or speed of aeroplanes; the deflection of classical references, a kind of transmutation of musical values; the mixture of unusual flavours – sausage and coffee; the use of products traditionally excluded from cooking – eau de cologne.

Marinetti's dietetic couplings are supposed to be revolutionary. They actualize (we shall see to what extent it is only a case of *reactualization*) unexpected marriages. This is how bananas go with anchovies and the sweet with the savoury. Thus 'The Tummy Tickler' recipe proposes 'a slice of pineapple on which sardines are laid out in rays. The centre of the pineapple slice is covered with a layer of tuna on which sits half a nut.'[15] The same for the mixture of meat and fish. Fillìa thus describes:

'Immortal Trout: Stuff some trout with chopped nuts and fry them in olive oil. Then wrap the trout in very thin slices of calves' liver.'[16] Finally, the Futurist cook does not hesitate to mingle different kinds of dishes – hors d'oeuvre and dessert in a 'Simultaneous Ice-cream' made of frozen cream and little pieces of raw onion.

Final provocations coming from the modernists are transgression and the taste of pure subjectivity. An example is 'Drunken Calf', for which this is the recipe: 'Fill some uncooked veal with chopped apples, nuts, pine nuts and cloves. Cook in the oven. Serve cold in a bath of Asti Spumante or Passito wine from Lipari.'[17] In the same way clams, garlic, onions, rice and vanilla cream are mixed to construct a dish called 'Gulf of Trieste'. More likely to disturb the religious orders and shock the chefs at the Vatican is the 'The Great Waters', a daring creation by the aeropainter Prampolini. It is a mixture of grappa, gin, kümmel and anise, on which 'float a square of anchovy paste wrapped pharmaceutically in a [communion] wafer'.[18] Professor Sirocofran will suggest even more perilous projects with his 'Prisoned Perfumes', which require a certain dexterity:

> Put a drop of perfume inside some thin brightly-coloured balloons. Blow them up and warm them gently to vaporise the perfume and swell the outer surface. Bring them to the table contemporaneously with the coffee, in little warmed dishes, making sure the perfumes are various. Hold a lighted cigarette near the bladders and inhale the scents that escape.[19]

Worth a try . . .

Linguistic novelty not only crops up in naming the plate as a whole, but characterizes the procedures for getting there, or the newly created arrangements in the Futurists' associations. The poetics of christening dishes is a culinary tradition – less usual is verbal invention describing the alchemy that leads to the plate. The Latinate prefix 'con', meaning *with* or *together*, allows for some new words: *conrumore* (with noise), *conluce* (with light), *conmusica* (with music), *conprofuma* (with smell) and *contatille* (with touch). All say something about the affinity between a sensation and a food. *Conrumore* is found at the union of rice in orange sauce and a motorcycle engine, hence the name of the dish: 'Roar on Ascent'. *Conluce* is present in the association of 'Excited Pig'/red lightning; *conmusica* with sculpted meat and musical ballet; while *conprofuma* characterizes the association of pulped potato and roses; and *contattile* the meeting of banana purée and velvet or a woman's skin.

Similarly, other words are formed with the prefix 'dis', meaning *apart*, so as to signal a dish and a sensation complementing each other: *disrumore* for 'Italian Sea' allied with the hiss of hot oil, or the bubbling of a gaseous liquid or sea foam; *disluce* for the pair formed by chocolate ice cream and hot orange light; *dismusica* for dates with anchovies and Beethoven's ninth symphony; *disprofuma* for the complementary aromas of raw meat and jasmine; and *distatille* for the tactile complementarity of 'Equator + North Pole' and sponge.

The vocabulary is also adapted to new dishes: a decision about a name has nothing to do with a previous meaning. If it does so it will be via the mouth, since the *decisione* refers to a 'hot-tonic *polibibite* [Marinetti's word for cocktail] that helps one to make, after a short but profound meditation, an important decision'.[20] *Guerrainletto* (war-in-bed) is the name for a *polibibite* inspiring fertility, *paceinletto* (peace-in-bed) a *polibibite* for inducing sleep and the *prestoinletto* (quick-to-bed) is 'a winter warming *polibibite*'.

Finally, culinary creations are named evocatively; the poetry of the menus is suggestive. 'The Bombardment of Adrianopolis' brings together eggs, olives, capers, anchovies, butter, rice and milk, skilfully combined then fried after being rolled into breadcrumbed balls. The Futurists' predilection for aircraft appears in a number of recipes: 'Roar on Ascent', already discussed – veal risotto à l'orange with marsala; 'Veal Fuselage' – slices of veal attached to a fuselage made of chestnuts, cooked onions covered in cocoa; 'Piquant Airport' – Russian salad, mayonnaise, green vegetables, bread rolls stuffed with orange, fruit, anchovies, sardines, and everything arranged in a field of greens in the form of cut-out aeroplanes in silhouette. And others – 'Libyan Aeroplane', 'Network in the Sky'. Here is a description of the 'Digestive Landing': 'Out of a sweet *potiglia* of chestnuts boiled in water and vanilla sticks form a landscape of mountains and plains. Above it, with blue ice cream, form atmospheric layers and streak them with aeroplanes of pastry coming down at an angle toward the ground.'[21] Sometimes one or another formula makes one think of Erik Satie's humorous titles for musical pieces; for example, 'Intuitive Veal', 'Milk in a Green Light', 'Italian Breasts in the Sunshine', 'Edible Skier', 'Zoological Soup' and 'Divorced Eggs'.

The actual meals are veritable happenings where humour rubs shoulders with fanatical experimentation. In an official meal that Marinetti wanted to be archetypal, he proposes a jester to amuse the guests with dirty jokes which, however, were supposed to avoid vulgarity. No instructions are given as to how to distinguish the two. Then a plate called 'Cannibals sign up at Geneva' is brought to the table. It is composed of diverse raw meats cut according to the fantasy of each person and seasoned by dipping in cups containing condiments like spices or wine. Then they serve 'The Society of Nations', a sort of custard with little black sausages and chocolate bars swimming in it. During the meal, 'a twelve-year-old Negro boy, hidden under the table, will tickle the ladies' legs and pinch their ankles'.[22] The meal finishes with a 'Solid Treaty', a kind of multi-coloured nougat cake full of tiny bombs, which on exploding would fill the room with the smell of battle. And after that, a cook babbles excuses for half an hour, asking that he be pardoned for having blown up a monumental dessert while on the job. Then, in the place of the vaunted destroyed edifice, a drunk arrives asking for a drink: 'A choice of the best Italian wines, of great quality and quantity, is lavished upon him, but on one condition, that he speak for two hours on possible solutions to the problem of disarmament, the revision of treaties and the financial crisis.'[23] We can be sure that this sardonic alimentary parody of democracy would not have displeased Mussolini, seduced as he was by the extreme modernity of the Futurists.

Marinetti provides a number of routines of the same stamp, halfway between mockery, humour and the serious will to transform values. There were economic meals, meals for love or weddings, bachelors or extremists filling up after two days of fasting, and other rituals: aeropoetic, tactile, geographical or sacred.

In fact, Marinetti's zealousness goes too far since he strives to situate dietetics far beyond the alimentary tradition. He takes modernity out of its tangled-up attachment to a fixed past; at least he thinks he does. However, quite a few of his transgressions are only resurrections of ancient or medieval practices. While aiming for culinary revolution, he ends up agitating for an alimentary reactionism.

Tracts on cooking from the second half of the seventeenth century provide evidence for the practice of associating sweet and savoury – as in fish with dates and preserved fruit, or strawberry soup. You only have to think about the subsequently famous duck à l'orange, or chicken with pineapple. Similarly, in Massialot's recipes of 1691 there are mixtures of meats and fish, significantly a duck with oysters. In 1739 Marin combines truffles, oysters and white veal. And finally, a glance around history teaches us that everywhere in the world people have always mixed up types of food. In Mexico, a traditional festive dish is made with goose and chocolate. In Spain, lobster and chicken is mixed in a stew of aromas, spices and chocolate – onion, cloves, celery, pepper, chilli, tomatoes, peanuts, garlic, salt and cocoa.

Today, everyone cooks wild game with fruit and cranberry sauce – venison with apples, and with gooseberry jelly. In Normandy, on the coast of the Channel, the Dieppois stew is a vast *pot-au-feu* with chicken and fish from the adjacent sea – land and sea combined.

The Futurist transgression that made carnations a suitable garnish for veal is echoed in vegetarian recipes that invite us to make daisy salads with hard-boiled eggs, just as one cooks the flowers of eggplants, nasturtiums, roses, acacias, violets and lavender.

Whatever is put forward as the latest in novelty, or a will to Copernican revolution, is nearly always the reactivation of some culinary past. The French Nouvelle Cuisine of the 1970s and '80s was quite often created on the premises of collectors of old cooking manuscripts. Hiding their sources, they rediscovered medieval preparations that were more surprising than anyone could imagine: John Dory fish fillet with gooseberries or strawberry soup are just two examples.

If there is no innocent dietetics, nor is there any profoundly revolutionary one. Everything has always already been prepared, ingested and eaten. The mouth is an historical site, and history is but an eternal recommencement. Dietetics reveals the eternal return.

SEVEN

Sartre; or, The Revenge of the Crustaceans

Sartre did not like crustaceans, and they did not like him any better. In *Adieux: A Farewell to Sartre*, Simone de Beauvoir questions the philosopher about his likes and dislikes in food. When asked about his strongest dislikes, Sartre responds: 'Crustaceans, oysters, shellfish'.[1] To justify his repugnance for these foods, he describes crustaceans as insects whose doubtful consciousness troubles him, as though they are almost entirely absent from this world: 'When I eat a crustacean, I am eating something that belongs to another world. That white flesh is not made for us, it is stolen from another universe'.[2] Pursuing this thought, Sartre says:

> It is food buried in an object, and you have to pry it out. It's mainly this notion of prying out that disgusts me. The fact that the creature is so snugly inside the shell that you have to use tools to get it out, rather than cutting it off. That's something that makes it seem allied to minerals.[3]

In the apprehension he feels about shellfish Sartre cannot separate the food from its nature – a quasi-vegetable form of existence, frankly related to the slimy, the viscous, for which he has expressed so much repugnance.[4] In the oyster, the cockle or the mussel, he sees 'organic life in the act of coming into being; or life which is only organic in the rather repulsive aspect of lymphatic flesh, strange colour, and a gaping hole in its substance'. Sartre laid the foundations for what might be called his metaphysics of the hole very early – in his *War Diaries* he borrows from Freudian theories that associate the hole with excretive and erotic pleasure. Prosaically, he treats the hole as the lack par excellence, which demands to be filled. He then argues with some care to show that 'the cult of the hole is anterior to that of the anus' and as it were plays leisurely with this hole, which occupies him for several pages.[5] In December 1939 the metaphysics of the 'holes-for-man' bypasses the problem of food, but its development in *Being and Nothingness* does not.[6]

In Sartre's masterpiece, *Being and Nothingness*, nutrition makes its appearance in the guise of a formal phenomenological analysis:

> [The tendency to fill] . . . is certainly one of the most funda-
> mental among those which serve as the basis for the act
> of eating; nourishment is the 'cement' which will seal the
> mouth; to eat is, among other things, to fill.[7]

Then follows the translation into philosophical jargon:

> Thus to plug up a hole means originally to make a sacrifice
> of my body in order that the plenitude of being may exist;
> that is, to subject the passion of the For-itself, so as to
> shape, to protect and to serve the totality of the In-itself.

Plugging up holes is eating as well as copulating, but if Sartre did not hesitate to write of 'the obscenity of the female sex organ',[8] he wrote nothing definitive about the mouth that eats, distinguishes flavours, associates aromas, sifts substances – whereas he analysed the sex that sucks in, engulfs, absorbs and grasps. The relationship between the two orifices is underlined in this way: 'Beyond any doubt her sex is a mouth, and a voracious mouth which devours the penis.'[9] But could you without difficulty transpose the terms of the proposition and see a sex in every mouth – if the quirks of grammar allow such a formulation? Probably.

Armed with Simone de Beauvoir's stories about Sartre, it is easy to approach an understanding of his diet. You can hear the echo of the equivalence between things of the sex and those of the mouth in his companion's statement that 'the sex act in the strict sense did not interest Sartre particularly.'[10] In *The Prime of Life* she writes: 'I criticised Sartre for regarding his body as a mere bundle of striated muscles, and for having cut it out of his emotional world.'[11]

Sartre's use of his body frankly betrays his contempt for the self and his repudiation of the flesh. The philosopher is fully, if unwillingly, in the Platonic tradition of the perfection of Ideas, of things of the mind, and disgust for the body – regarded as a tomb, a maleficent box containing the principle of perfection. An intellectual with his head in the clouds, the career of the existential philosopher evolves in a complete absence of hygiene. Nothing says more about him than this abandonment of the self to the vagaries of corrupted matter. The anecdotes about Sartre's dirtiness tell of his faculty for forgetting the flesh, for despising it and restricting it to the category of the superfluous. In Germany he had allowed filth and stench to reach the point that his biographer could speak of his 'pestilential room', and weeks would pass 'without taking a bath when all he had to do was cross the street and pay ten sous to have exclusive use of a bathroom in the heated building.'[12] His nickname at that time was 'the man with the black gloves, because his hands were black with dirt up to his elbows.'[13]

Bodily needs always inspired disgust and contempt in Sartre. Beauvoir confides that he always relieved himself discreetly as long as his health held up. Afterwards, when the decomposition of the thinker was plain, he demonstrated a fatalism that astonished his companion. Incontinent on armchairs and sofas, he showed no modesty, only resignation.

Oblivious of hygiene, Sartre was also oblivious of the rhythms of the body and the need to transcend natural necessity with the cultural rituals of the meal. The quantity and quality of his meals were deplorable, matched by the frequency of his sacrifices to the rite: 'I don't at all mind missing the midday meal, or even both main meals; eating just bread, or alternatively salad with no bread; or actually fasting for a day or two.'[14] Beauvoir confirms that he would eat anything, anytime, anywhere.[15]

The contempt for his own body was accompanied, naturally enough, by a contempt for the body in general. In his analysis of this essential reality in *Being and Nothingness*, he furnishes an endless array of telling examples – sore legs, eyes dissected by surgeons, a body destroyed by a bomb, a broken arm, a dead body, gastralgia, headaches, pains in the stomach, the fingers and the eyes.[16] The body as being-for-itself: facticity. The body in Sartre is above all sick, mutilated, butchered, unrecognizable. Not a body enjoying the pleasures of the table or sensuality, of joyful flesh or frissons of pleasure, but one that is sick, spoiled or decaying. Meticulous with detail, Sartre develops his conceptions of nausea and vomiting, and to this end he calls upon 'putrid meat, fresh blood, excrement'. Likewise, he discourses on a stomach ulcer perceived as 'a gnawing, a slight internal putrescence; I can conceive of it by means of analogy with abscesses, fever blisters, pus, canker sores etc.'[17] The modalities of being-for-others mediated by the body are not the smile, the seductive look, but sweat and body odour. The metaphors of the body are spun out by spiders, the face of the other inspires nausea; his own face even allows him a witticism about 'disgust with [his] too-white flesh'.[18] A tool for using tools, the body is nothing but a machine, without desire or a drive to pleasure.

With Sartre the contempt for the self, the use of the self as a thing, is presented under the two aspects of alcohol and tobacco – variations on the theme of the horror of the self. Annie Cohen-Solal draws up the account of Sartre's consumption during a day:

two packets of Boyard cigarettes and numerous pipes stuffed with dark tobacco; more than a litre of alcohol (wine, beer, vodka, whisky etc.); two hundred milligrams of amphetamines; fifteen grams of aspirin; several grams of barbiturates; not counting the coffees, teas and heavy meals that made up his daily diet.[19]

The Critique of Dialectical Reason, written after Being and Nothingness, was created at the price of more than a tube of corydrane (a mixture of aspirin and amphetamines) per day.

There is no doubt about Sartre's alcoholism. His bouts of drunkenness punctuate the memoirs of Simone de Beauvoir. The most celebrated of these occurred in Moscow, earning him ten days of hospitalization in the spring of 1954. Sympathetic biographers blame the importuning of his Soviet hosts. After a medical consultation, when Sartre realized that he would have to finish with alcohol, he cried: 'It's sixty years of my life that I'm saying goodbye to.'[20]

Between tubes of corydrane Sartre performed a phenomenological analysis of alcoholism. He wrote:

Thus it amounts to the same thing whether one gets drunk alone or is a leader of nations. If one of these activities takes precedence over the other, this will not be because of its real goal, but because of the degree of consciousness which it possesses of its ideal goal; and in this case it will be the quietism of the solitary drunkard which will take precedence over the vain agitation of the leader of nations.[21]

Perhaps he wanted to demonstrate his theory; in any case in 1973 – the year he was told to stop drinking – he confided to a journalist from *Actuel* his whole political programme, which can be summed up in three words: terror, illegality and armed violence.

> A revolutionary regime must get rid of a certain number of individuals that threaten it and I see no other means for this than death; it is always possible to get out of a prison; the revolutionaries of 1793 probably didn't kill enough people.[22]

The least of the problems of alcoholism . . .

The medical consultation of 1973 had also brought to light a cerebral anoxia, an asphyxiation of the brain. His arteries and arterioles were in a parlous state. Alcohol was a major contributor, as was tobacco. In *Being and Nothingness*, Sartre puts forward a little theory about smoking – to smoke is to practise a ceremony, to theatricalize your movements, to ritualize them. It is also 'an appropriative, destructive action'. Tobacco is a symbol of 'appropriated' being, since it is destroyed in the rhythm of my breathing in a mode of 'continuous destruction', since it passes into me and its change in myself is manifested symbolically by the transformation of the consumed solid into smoke. In its scale, this 'crematory sacrifice', as Sartre calls it, plays out a sacrifice of all humanity, 'destructively appropriating the entire world. Across the tobacco which I was smoking was the world which was burning, which was going up in smoke, which was being reabsorbed into vapour so as to re-enter into me.'[23] Smoking and eating are two forms of a single logic. But tobacco seems to be a handy substitute for food – a substitute that is magical, insubstantial, evanescent, with an almost neutral flavour due to its astringent effect on the taste buds.

Stimulants – alcohol and tobacco – are not enough for Sartre's arsenal of gentle self-mutilation. As a statement of his distanced use of his body, the experiment with mescaline is not without interest. His declared reason for the mescaline experiment was philosophical – he hoped to measure on himself its effect on the formation of images in an individual. He asked for assistance from Dr Lagache from Sainte-Anne hospital. A dose calculated to produce effects from between four and twelve hours was injected under medical supervision. He analysed the effects in *The Psychology of the Imagination*.[24] Beauvoir described the hallucinations that Sartre reported to her: 'on his sides, from behind, swarmed crabs and polyps and grimacing Things'.[25] Revenge of the crustaceans. Sartre believed he was being chased by lobsters. When in a phone call Beauvoir expressed concern about the progress of the experiment, Sartre replied in a confused voice that her 'phone call had wrenched him away from a fight with octopuses which he certainly wouldn't have won'. Triumph of the catch . . . Later, in the street, even though mescaline does not produce flashbacks, Sartre found himself 'really convinced that there was a lobster trotting along behind him'.[26] Beauvoir did not believe it was an effect of the hallucinogen, but that the philosopher suffered from a nervous disorder quite unrelated to his experience at Sainte-Anne. Sartre would remember this bestiary, which in his case was highly symbolic, when in *Nausea* he made Roquentin an intimate of an aquatic zoo, housing animals '[whose] bodies were made of slices of toast, such as you put under roast pigeon; they were walking sideways with crablike legs'.[27]

The recurrence of crustaceans is conspicuous in Sartre's works. In *Words* he tells how as a child he came across an illustration in the Hachette almanac that showed a moonlit quay, where a long jagged claw emerged from the water, grabbed a drunkard, and dragged him down into the sea-green depths. The text illustrated by this image concludes with: 'Was it a drunkard's hallucination? Had hell gaped? I was afraid of water, of crabs, and of trees' – remember the role of the root in *Nausea*. Intensifying the impression of this sinister illustration, Sartre confides that he often replayed the terrifying scene in his room, in the evening shadows. He states that dramatization requires a subterranean or undersea place from which The Being surged in the shape of an aquatic or chthonic creature: 'an octopus with fiery eyes, a twenty-ton crustacean, or a giant talking spider – was myself, a childish monster; it was my boredom with life, my fear of death, my vapidity and my perversity.'[28] Similarly, in *The Condemned of Altona*, crabs appear and provide the pretext for an exchange between two characters, one of whom predicts the accession of the Decapods to the top ranks of human beings: 'They'll have different bodies', he says, 'and therefore different ideas.'[29] But the crustaceans have only a modest victory; they do not become embedded in the theoretical works, at least as objects of existential psychoanalysis. They play only secondary roles, as illustrations, accompanists for the music. The exacting phenomenologist of the alimentary knows that one's relation to food is one's relation to the world. His analyses bear on the whole world. But he has a blind spot in this regard. Popular wisdom invokes the mote and the beam to speak of such matters. In *Being and Nothingness* he writes:

> It is not a matter of indifference whether we like oysters or clams, snails or shrimp, if only we knew how to unravel the existential significance of these foods. Generally speaking there is no irreducible taste or inclination. They all represent a certain appropriate choice of being. It is up to existential psychoanalysis to compare and classify them.[30]

Tell me what you eat . . .

Sartre admits there are not many things he likes to eat. Apart from his frank repugnance for seafood, he confesses to a pronounced distaste for tomatoes, rejecting their acid flesh. In general, he does not care for what he calls 'vegetables', even though they carry a lower degree of consciousness than shell-fish. He never eats fruits in their natural state: they are guilty of being products of chance and too distant from the human. The philosopher confesses his preference for fruit integrated into a human preparation – so, pastries. He will accept food only after it has been technically or culturally mediated by humans. Anti-Diogenes par excellence, he abhors nature and finds only manufactured, artificial products to his liking: 'Food must be the result of work performed by men. Bread is like that. I've always thought that bread was a relation with other men.'[31]

He ate meat for a long time, but dropped it for reasons close to the hearts of vegetarians – to eat meat is to devour dead bodies. To Beauvoir's question, 'What do you like then?' Sartre responds:

Certain things among the various kinds of meat and veg-etables. Eggs too. I used to be very fond of *charcuterie*, but I like it less now. It seemed to me that there man was using meat to make something entirely new – an andouillette, for example, an andouille, a sausage. All these existed through the agency of man. The blood has been taken out in a certain manner, then treated in a certain manner. The cooking was carried out in a clearly defined fashion dis-covered by men. The sausage was given a shape that I found tempting, with little bits of string at either end.[32]

Charcuterie requires a transformation, a modification of the raw material: blood, flesh, fat – it is the alchemy that transmutes the crude material of its elements, the unity you reach after a coded series of cultural and artisanal operations. The andouille as Sartre's emblem, where that of Diogenes is the raw octopus . . . red meat, even when it is cooked, remains full of blood. But, Sartre continues, 'A sausage or an andouille is not like that. The sausage, with its white specks and round pink flesh, is quite another thing.'[33]

Towards the end of his life Sartre abandoned his ritual meals at La Coupole at lunchtime, and anywhere with Beauvoir in the evenings. He admitted to making do with 'a slice of pâté or something like that' for dinner.[34] Insensitivity of the lips, missing teeth and senility (exacerbated by his failing eyesight) all led to Sartre ending up smearing his face with sauces and food, while vehemently refusing any assistance. Sartre's meals were heavy, 'rich in charcuteries, sauerkraut dishes and chocolate cakes, all washed down with a litre of wine'.[35] He ate nuts and almonds, although they hurt his tongue, and he admitted to liking pineapple – though a fruit – because it seemed to him to be like something cooked.

'All food is a symbol', he says.[36] Honey, molasses and sugar are in his eyes associated with the viscous. Recalling the correspondences of the symbolists, Sartre takes us to a strange synaesthesia: 'If I eat a pink cake, the taste of it is pink; the light sugary perfume, the oiliness of the butter cream *are* the pink. Thus I eat the pink as I see the sugary.'[37] Sartre played this game of unexpected symmetries during their trip to Italy; for example, he compares 'the palaces of Genoa with the taste and colour of Italian cakes'.[38] Sartre's associations would be worthy of an existential psychoanalysis – that is the least one could do for their originator. The taste of the viscous, of the doughy, of the oily, the stodgy, the dense, the liquid – all that is highly significant.

Nausea is apprehended under the form of the pallid, the limp, the tepid and the sticky, whereas the transcendence of contingency and facticity calls for the dark, the hard and the cold. Desire in Sartre is mineralization, fossilization and escape from corruptible categories. With a resurgence of Platonism, Sartre understands the real as a partition between the immediate and the essential, between what emerges and what is submerged. Outside of water is appearance – illusion formed from images, roots, things. Under the water is the truth of being and the authentic nature of the world:

> And *under* the water? Haven't you thought about what there may be *under* the water? A monster, a huge carapace half-embedded in the mud. A dozen pairs of claws slowly furrow the slime. The monster raises itself a little, every now and then. At the bottom of the water.[39]

Such teratological visions tell us a lot about the person who imagined them – the real is only perceptions, and perceptions are the responsibility of the subject. There is only a relativity of sensations, images, tastes:

> Quality – particularly a material quality like the fluidity of water or the density of stone – is a mode of being and so can only present being in one certain way. What we choose is a certain way in which being reveals itself and lets itself be possessed. The yellow and the red, the taste of tomato or split peas, the coarse and the tender, are by no means irreducible givens according to our view: for us they translate symbolically a certain form in which being appears, and we react by disgust or desire according to how we see being rise up in one way or another to their surface.[40]

Taste is a pathway to subjectivity, one of the lines converging towards individual reality, a fragment with the memory of the whole, shedding light on the subject's conception of the world. Each being gives salty, sweet, bitter a symbolic charge that identifies it as a singular project. Sartre describes the strange alchemy that is carried out in each being during the crystallization of synaesthesia. The story of correspondences – the investigation of their mode of formation, the creation of their meanings – lies in the province of existential psychoanalysis.

What is . . . the metaphysical coefficient of lemon, of water, of oil etc.? Psychoanalysis must resolve all these problems if it wants to understand some day why Pierre likes oranges and has a horror of water, why he gladly eats tomatoes and refuses to eat beans, why he vomits if he is forced to swallow oysters, or raw eggs.[41]

From the likes and dislikes of a being, one can attain to its truth understood as a:

free project of the unique person in terms of the individual relationship which unites him to these various symbols of being . . . In this way tastes do not remain irreducible givens; if one knows how to question them, they reveal to us the fundamental projects of the person. Down to even our alimentary preferences they all have a meaning. We can account for this fact if we will reflect that each taste is presented, not as an absurd datum which we must excuse but as an evident value. If I like the taste of garlic, it seems irrational to me that other people can not like it. To eat is to appropriate by destruction; it is at the same time to be filled up with a certain being.[42]

Following this are several lines in which the evocation of a chocolate biscuit that resists, gives way and crumbles, accords with the conclusions of the analysis.

Sartre gives away a lot in *Words*. Among other things he confesses that ugliness was his first mode of being-in-the-world – this revelation coming to him as he left a hairdressing appointment. The child was first perceived by others as a batrachian with a complex about his small size and his puny and sickly appearance – 'a weakling who interested no one'.[43] He was not allowed into groups and others' games, and he suffered from it. The rest is only allusion . . . Can we not see here the beginnings of the founding project of his whole biography, and the premise on which the rest of his life was constructed? Appropriating the exclusion that had been forced on him by others, Sartre turns himself into a crab.[44] As a conclusion to his life, one could cite the following: 'All of a sudden, I lost the appearance of a man and they saw a crab escaping backwards from that all-too-human room. Now the unmasked intruder has fled: the show goes on.'[45] Sartre being pursued by a lobster is the walker being joined by his image, his shadow – shellfish are not to be despised lightly – beware the man who lacks respect for the lobster.

Conclusion:
The Gay Science of Eating

Exhausted, done in and well fed, the six philosophers bring their banquet to an end, leaving behind the remnants of a significant meal. Diogenes has reminded us that we cannot make Nature our guiding principle without a thorough understanding of food. Holding aloft an octopus, he once more speaks of the Cynical demand for simplicity, and the rejection of the sophisticated, the complex and the civilized. After hosing down every fire he can reach with a great stream of urine – like his *confrère* at the dinner of Lucian of Samosata – the philosopher of the amphora denounces once again the Promethean dimension at work in the real. Nothing good is to be found outside the natural, he explains. Convinced by the brilliance of his excoriating speech, he grabs the human flesh that is lying on the ground and sits down, giving the floor to the next speaker.

Close by, looking interested and a little neurasthenic, Rousseau rises to speak. He begins by citing points of agreement with his predecessor – the rejection of the complex, praise of the simple, the will of nature. But he also recalls his opposition in principle to eating any flesh – whether cooked or raw. Milk will always suffice for those who turn away from the world. Plebeian to the point of caricature, the citizen of Geneva extols the virtues of a life modelled on the movements of a nature raised to the mythical level of perfection. Fantasizing about Sparta, Rousseau develops a theory of food somewhat reminiscent of the social contract – asceticism and sobriety, the absence of whimsy and chance.

A dream of order with simple machines with uncomplicated mechanisms. The virtues of kindness, milk and nature are promoted over cruelty, meat and civilization. The dream against reality. It does not take much for such a fantasy to become reality. In 1789 the bloody proponents of a vegetarianism raised to the level of a republican virtue violently led their citizens to a spartan diet and political forms. The Lacaedemonian model as the outcome for modernity – there is plenty there to trouble a Voltairian adherent of the free circulation of ideas, and plump young chickens.

Like a good student, silent and keen to learn, Kant is taking notes with a glass in his hand. He has been keenly savouring the speech of the Genevan. Kant regards a little alcohol as the best way to promote and maintain the conviviality and ambience of banquets. Less of the *syssitia* and more of the feast. Re-reading his notes, he concludes that some of Rousseau's analyses are cogent. In the pedagogical, anthropological and historical texts of the old master of Königsberg can be found overt echoes of *Emile* and some other works of the Swiss. We can be surprised to find Kant, whom we would expect to be sober, austere and pathologically hypochondriac, dead drunk in the streets of his Prussian city. Königsberg is now the Russian city Kaliningrad. No doubt, in this Russian province, Kant's habit of occasionally staggering around the streets of the port at night has been kept up.

At the turn of the century, with the French and industrial revolutions, we would have had to say something about Brillat-Savarin or indeed Grimod de La Reynière. The former is rather sceptical and questioning, even at the table, because he is writing a book – *The Physiology of Taste* – which is at once philosophical, sensualist and literary. Condillac and Maine de Biran are not far off. The gastronome's analysis draws on multiple disciplines: physiology, medicine, chemistry and hygiene, and sometimes geography or ethics. Brillat-Savarin opens up the era of writers whose focus is food. That is true. But it is also through him that pleasure is no longer seen to be something shameful. The book clearly stakes its success on eudemonia, endlessly arguing for the superiority of pleasure. He creates its theory, its logic and its poetics. Tasty brother-in-law of Charles Fourier, he is the philosopher who dared to think about the senses, and particularly about taste. Before him we might wonder whether philosophers have a nose and a palate;[1] sometimes even whether they are simple machines devoid of senses – insensate in fact – automatons like those of Vaucanson, with no more passion than cogs and gears. Brillat-Savarin is the heir to a rather discreet, though effective tradition – that of the sensualists, the libertines, the epicureans of the Grand Siècle, the materialists. He also opens new perspectives on a manifest modernity. Forced to name names, one would have to offer Ludwig Feuerbach, Arthur Schopenhauer and Friedrich Nietzsche. All three of these are contemptuous of the spiritualism/materialism dualism, but are also proponents of an immanent logic that works to integrate the forces, powers and vitality of a desiring machine. Equally how could we forget that, closer to us, the reflections of Deleuze and Guattari almost carry the ideas of La Mettrie to their definitive expression – or rather the ideas of a La Mettrie who had known Freud?[2]

We can be sure that at the philosophers' banquet we have discovered Brillat-Savarin and Grimod de La Reynière are guests, but also La Mettrie, Sade, Margaret Mary, Gassendi, Saint-Evremond and La Mothe Le Vayer. And most likely Gaston Bachelard and Michel Serres are also in attendance.

The encounter between Margaret Mary and Sade takes place in a singular fashion. Ironically, chance has seated them face-to-face, like the symbolic expressions of two antagonistic tendencies. Strange . . . and in close proximity to the saint and the libertine we can find the fantastic and bewildering reasoning of the Gnostics – those fanatics of the desert who reject the flesh, the body. In a corner of the feast they prefer to pray. Stylites, Gyrovagues or grazers – these are the pathways to a Christianity that condemns skin, blood, meat and lymph; they are too vulgar. The cycle of ingestion/digestion, eating/defecating is for them the clearest sign of subjection to the contingent. Their model was Jesus, of whom Valentinus wrote: 'he eats and drinks, but does not defecate. The power of his continence was such that foodstuffs did not corrupt in him, since there was no corruption in him.'[3]

Let us return to Margaret Mary – a saint of the Grand Siècle – and the psychoanalyst who looked into her case. This psycho-analyst was, moreover, René Major, a specialist in the delirium associated with nominative determinism.[4] He pointed out that the saint's lay name was Alacoque ('soft-boiled egg' in French). Seriously. We can also note that above all she hated cheese and that she put it to a mystical use, since she forced herself to eat it in spite of her repugnance.[5] On her menu: multiple mortifi-cations, denial of basic bodily imperatives, pleasure in contempt of the self, discipline, hair shirts, flagellation, lack of defecation (an obsession with the ecstatics) and refusal of food. Her pref-erence, when she deigned to eat anything, was for foods that were marginal – to say the least! You be the judge; she particularly enjoyed the bitter potions prescribed by her doctor.[6] The more disgusting the taste, the longer she put off swallowing, and the more she savoured it. She also ate 'the food that a sick person was unable to keep down; and another time, while caring for a nun with dysentery [she touched] with her tongue the very thing that turned her stomach.'[7] When a plate was dropped on the ground and the meal was thrown in the dirt, she kept the dirtiest morsels for herself.[8]

Happily, her chance companion, the divine Marquis de Sade, is at the same banquet. For the saint, eating is a way of fulfilling the contempt of the self; for the libertine it is an argument for the expansion of desires and pleasures. The familiar of the

Bastille, the man with sweets plates filled with cantharides-flavoured treats, has a remarkable appetite. Carefully drafting the standing rules of the Society of the Friends of Crime, he writes (in Article 16): 'Every excess of eating and drinking is authorized . . . every possible measure is furnished to satisfy them.'[9] As always with erotomaniacs, food is subjected to sex – it restores the body from sexual exertion or prepares for it. In contrast to the mystics, who call for abstinence, de Sade incites excess – feasts, orgies and culinary celebrations are combined. Every moment of sexual initiation is celebrated through eating. The Sadeian religion of the digestive drink celebrates the two terms of this dialectic – ingestion/defecation. Faeces is sanctified in the marquis' theory of gastronomy; it is the teleological moment of nutrition.

Missing from the fanatics of ecstasy, faeces could not be more present among the sensualists. The geography of excrement as it appears in the *120 Days of Sodom* is suggestive in this respect. The platitude whereby extremities meet in the end is verified by lining up the gnostic or religious experiences of Margaret Mary with those of de Sade. Let Noëlle Châtelet provide the catalogue:

> Turning through the pages . . . you will note with growing discomfort the succession of unexpected ingestions, from snot to embryos, by way of saliva, pus, sperm, farts, menstrual blood, tears, belches, pre-chewed food, and vomit.[10]

Nothing is wasted.

Who among those invited to the banquet could match him for omnivorousness? Diogenes perhaps. It is true that the Marquis' interests in food are a bit like those of Diogenes – not so much natural as counter-cultural or anti-cultural. He transgresses alimentary prohibitions in order to profit from libertarian ingestion. Nothing can contain or limit its possibilities. In the kingdom of Sadean festivity, nothing is prohibited. This is how coprophagy, murder or cannibalism can come into the picture.[11] And equally where vampire-like practices come from, and other scenarios that meet the needs of hematophagic desire. And also, finally, the consumption of roasted little girl or even – to refer to Noëlle Châtelet for the list: testicle pâté, human blood sausage, turd sorbet, etc.[12] Perverse, writes this shocked reader. She should reread Klossowski, Lély or Blanchot.

Sade is more talk than action. The information gleaned from his fiction must be balanced against that found in his biography and correspondence, especially his letters to his wife. Libertarianism is his concern. He does not encourage debauchery, because he knows that should it take place, it will do so necessarily. He does not encourage anthropophagy, but asserts that if it exists, it can only be a part of nature, of natural necessity. Well before Nietzsche, Sade asserts a reading of reality as a logic submitted to determinism. In *Justine; or, The Misfortunes of Virtue,* he writes:

> Therefore, if there exist beings in the world whose tastes shock all accepted standards, not only should we not be astonished by them, not only should we not preach to them or punish them, but we should serve their interests, make them happy, abolish all restraints upon them, and if we wish to be just, provide them with every means to satisfy themselves without risk, because it was not more their choice to have strange tastes than it was yours to be witty or stupid, to have a fine figure or be a hunchback.[13]

Amor fati. Against nature nothing is possible . . .

Instead of a meal made of roast little girls and glacéd turds, Sade is happy with a quite innocent cuisine. The food of the fictional texts is imaginary, that of the letters is real. The food of fantasies knows no prohibitions, just as dreams know no limits. The favourite foods of this devourer of children are fowl, mincemeat, stewed fruit, marshmallow, sweets, spices, sweet milky treats, jams, meringues and chocolate cakes. Play lunch for a good little girl. Fresh meat has scarcely any attraction for him and he occasionally enjoys the refinements of champagne and truffles. A letter to his wife reveals the secrets of Sadean gastronomy:

> A bouillon made from twenty-four small sparrows, with rice and saffron. A pie with meatballs made from minced pigeon meat and garnished with artichoke bottoms. A vanilla cream. Truffles à la Provençale. A turkey stuffed with truffles. Eggs in gravy. Mince made from the white meat of partridge stuffed with truffles and fortified wine. Wine from Champagne. A compote perfumed with ambergris.[14]

Sade lives more on the margins through writing, in his novels, than through eating, in daily life. Would you prefer an invitation from Margaret Mary or Sade? The former, Alacoque, is more startling at the table – if one may say so – than the citizen-marquis. Instead of the blood of a prepubescent on his lips, the only traces Sade has on the corners of his mouth are the remains of the cocoa on his favourite cakes. The same cannot be said of the brown marks around the mouth of the saint.

Charles Fourier, his head in the clouds, as oblivious of his neighbours' monstrous writing as he is of their shop-girl behaviour, makes a case for a poetics of food. Copulation of stars to produce fruit, gastrosophical wars, a dialectic of the pie and a rhetoric of the vol-au-vent, the utopian rhapsodizes about kitchens as much as factories. Engrossed by a mythical Harmony, Fourier does not overlook food in his desire to lock down every aspect of the real. Fanatical about green plants to the point of living in an apartment converted into a greenhouse – the floor of his house was covered in soil – this philosopher of the new order put as much effort into developing his gastronomic ideas as in specifying his political thought or the details of his political economy. It is true that gastrosophy is a pivotal science. On his credit side, Fourier's genuine concern to change one's relationship to the body must be acknowledged. His main aim was the removal of guilt, and his first desire was living utopia to the full. Harmony is the political form given to joy.

Nose in the stars, Fourier does not see Nietzsche slaving away like a drudge. Several hours – up to ten – every day. He knows the path he follows by heart. His eyesight is too poor for him to be able to improvise with confidence. Mountain tracks are dangerous. Nietzsche's relationship with food tells us everything about the man and the philosopher. He produced a wonderful *oeuvre* in which some arguments are nevertheless mired in resentment. He wanted to have a partner or friend, and, disappointed by his fruitless wait, launched into misogynist and misanthropist diatribes. Zarathustra advocates taking a whip on each visit to a woman, but his master and creator intervened with the authorities to support the right of a woman to submit her doctorate – something that was not allowed at the time. Similarly, he confided an idea or two by way of letter to some women, such as Malvida von Meysenburg. It was the same with the friendship with Gast that was so reviled by Zarathustra, and was such an important part of Nietzsche's life: without Gast there would never have been a great Nietzschean *oeuvre* because of the shocking state of his eyesight. Peter Gast read and re-read, corrected and edited the definitive manuscripts for the author to approve. He took in Nietzsche in Venice, and came to his aid whenever he needed help. What is this if not friendship? Notwithstanding, he sees any special kind of relationship as a prison. Do we need another example? The success that he awaits in vain generates the resentment that makes him declare that he is writing for future generations, for the next century. You could say the same thing about food.

He rejects German heaviness and related foods, but only to throw himself into incoherent practices to do with some Piedmontese fantasy. He is interested in light-footedness and dance, so is fond of meats with sauce and pasta, but then he confines himself to the practicalities of his mother's sausages.

Marinetti pushes the consequences further. Futurist theory is put into practice. Marinetti's banquets really took place – as kitsch works of art, baroque scenarios. They were eloquent and energetic in their will to give the real a form starting from the pure moment in time, with all the residue of the past removed. Futurist gastronomy is seeking a culinary revolution, even if, here as elsewhere – in the way of these things – revolution turns into reaction. Once again the laws of history govern the saga of food. The history of alimentation is history pure and simple. The determination of a gastronomic sensibility or an eating behaviour is purely and simply the determination of a sensibility or a behaviour.

Finally, with Sartre, food designates the philosopher as the eternal enemy of his body. At one point his alcoholism is in competition with a Russian engineer in Tashkent, the next with Hemingway at the Ritz. He ends up sleeping it off in the lifeboat that was the liner taking him from Le Havre to New York. When in Japan he had a taste of raw bream or bloody tuna he vomited at the end of the meal. At the house of a Maoist miner in Bruay-en-Artois, he is served a jugged rabbit for dinner that brings on a two-hour asthma crisis. In Morocco he has terrible indigestion after eating *pastilla*, chicken *au citron*, *mechoui*, couscous and the marrow of gazelle's horns.[15] And one evening he experiences deafness for several hours because he took some amphetamine tablets. Let us leave him in his blessed silence, and let us be wary of any philosophies that make you deaf.

Food for nothingness and for eternity, humans are destined to ingest and be ingested. Death, as an alimentary metaphor, is but one of many versions of orality. Psychoanalysts have much to say on gastronomic oppositions: stage fixation, oral pleasure, cultural and socially acceptable substitutes for weaning, sublimation defined by the ephemeral. Psychiatrists analyse anorexia and bulimia in order to discover both sides of the same failing obsession to get a grip on the world. They make peremptory distinctions between the normal and the pathological, good and bad deviations in the use of the mouth. Economists talk, along with historians, about the poetic geography of condiments, the travels of sugars and caviar, the saga of salt. Along the way, they extract a theory. From the mastery of the sphincter to the banknote, paper money to precious shellfish. Mythological meanderings. They just need a Lewis Carroll or a Lucian of Samosata. Sociologists like Bourdieu talk about working-class predilections (heavy, salty, fatty) and middle-class preferences. Gastronomers talk about flavours, colours and savours, sapidity and melting or tender characteristics. But theologians would talk of one of their seven capital sins.

Then the philosopher might suggest eradicating the sacred, and annihilating the impulses to renunciation and asceticism we have integrated so thoroughly. Dionysian wisdom will point out the impertinence of secular praise and the barrenness of bringing Christianity to account. Atheist knowledge is aesthetic wisdom. Confusing a science of action with an art of living calls for a dietet(h)ics along eudemonic lines. The flesh has no destiny but to exist prior to death, since afterwards it is destined to rot and to burst into myriad pieces. The misuse of the body is a failing that contains its own sanction – lost time cannot be regained.

References

INTRODUCTION: THE BANQUET OF THE OMNIVORES

1 These points are covered in the following chapters.
2 Dimitri Davidenko, *Descartes le scandaleux* (Paris, 1988), p. 52.
3 Jean Colerus, 'The Life of B. de Spinoza', in *Spinoza: His Life and Philosophy*, trans. Frederick Pollock (London, 1880), p. 419 [translation modified].
4 G.W.F. Hegel, *Briefe von und an Hegel*, ed. Joseph Hoffmeister (Hamburg, 1952), p. 63.
5 Lydia Flem, *La vie quotidienne de Freud et de ses patients* (Paris, 1986): see pp. 238–40 for Freud, wines, wild berries, artichokes, asparagus and corncobs.
6 Noëlle Châtelet, 'La libertin au table', in *Sade: Ecrire la crise. Actes du colloque de Cérisy*, ed. Philippe Roger and Michel Camus (Paris, 1983).
7 André Castelot, *L'histoire à table* (Paris, 1979).
8 Claude Lévi-Strauss, *Tristes tropiques,* trans. John Russell (New York, 1971), p. 173.
9 Jacques Lacarrière, *The Gnostics*, trans. Nina Rootes (London, 1977), p. 70.
10 Pierre Clastres, *Chronicle of the Guayaki Indians*, trans. Paul Auster (New York, 1998), p. 341.
11 Julien Offray de La Mettrie, *L'art de jouir* (Potsdam, 1751), p. 61.

12 Julien Offray de La Mettrie, 'Man a Machine', in *Man a Machine and Man a Plant*, trans. Richard A. Watson and Maya Rybalka (Indianapolis, IN, and Cambridge, MA, 1994), p. 33.

13 Davidenko, *Descartes*, p. 105; Adrien Baillet, *La vie de Monsieur Descartes* (Paris, 2012); Elisabeth Badinter and Robert Badinter, *Condorcet* (Paris, 1989).

14 Ludwig Feuerbach, *Manifestes philosophiques: textes choisis, 1839–1845*, trans. Louis Althusser (Paris, 1960), p. 227.

15 Ludwig Feuerbach, *Pensées diverses* (Paris, 1987), pp. 327 and 336.

16 Noëlle Châtelet, *Le corps à corps culinaire* (Paris, 1998); Jean-Paul Aron, *Le mangeur du XIXe siècle* (Paris, 1976); Jean-François Revel, *Un festin en paroles* (Paris, 1982).

17 Michel Foucault, *The Use of Pleasure* (London, 1991), p. 97.

18 Ibid., p. 101.

19 Ibid., p. 108.

20 J. A. Brillat-Savarin, *The Physiology of Taste*, trans. M.F.K. Fisher (New York and London, 2009), p. 15.

21 Didier Raymond, *Schopenhauer* (Paris, 1997), p. 37.

1 DIOGENES; OR, THE TASTE OF OCTOPUS

1 Hegel, *Lectures on the Philosophy of History*, trans. E. S. Haldane (London, 1892), pp. 485, 487.

2 Friedrich Nietzsche, *Beyond Good and Evil*, trans. R. J. Hollingdale (Harmondsworth, 1973), p. 124.

3 Friedrich Nietzsche, *Ecce Homo*, trans. Walter Kaufmann (New York and Toronto, 1969), p. 281.

4 Ibid., p. 264.

5 Attributed to Plato by Diogenes Laërtius, *Lives of the Eminent Philosophers*, trans. R. D. Hicks (London and

New York, 1925), p. 6; Michel de Montaigne, *Essays*, trans. and ed. M. A. Screech (London, 1991), pp. 1258–9.

6 Diogenes Laërtius, *Lives*, p. 57.

7 Marcel Detienne, *Dionysos Slain*, trans. Mireille Muellner and Leonard Muellner (Baltimore, MD, and London, 1979), p. 64.

8 Marcel Detienne, 'Culinary Practices and the Spirit of Sacrifice', in *The Cuisine of Sacrifice Among the Greeks*, ed. Marcel Detienne and Jean-Paul Vernant, trans. Paula Wissing (Chicago and London, 1989), p 8.

9 Detienne, *Dionysos Slain*, p. x.

10 Detienne, 'Culinary Practices and the Spirit of Sacrifice', in *The Cuisine of Sacrifice*. See also J.-P. Vernant, 'At Man's Table', in ibid., p. 38.

11 Diogenes Laërtius, *Lives*, p. 75.

12 Plato, *The Republic*, trans. Robin Waterfield (Oxford, 1993), p. 307. See also pp. 308, 313 and 377.

13 *The Works of Lucian of Samosata*, trans. H. W. Fowler and F. G. Fowler (Oxford, 1905), IV, p. 179.

14 Dio Chrysostom, 'The Sixth Discourse: Diogenes; or, On Tyranny', in *Discourses 1–11*, trans. J. W. Colhoon (Cambridge, MA, 1932), p. 259.

15 Diogenes Laërtius, *Lives*, p. 47.

16 Dio Chrysostom, 'The Sixth Discourse', p. 65.

17 Diogenes, 'Lettre à Monime', in Léonce Paquet, *Les cyniques grecs* (Ottawa, 1988), XXXVII, p. 46.

18 Ibid.

19 Diogenes, *Lives*, p. 47.

20 Ibid., p. 59.

21 Plutarch, 'De esu carnium I', in *Plutarch's Moralia*, vol. XII, trans. Harold Cherniss and William C. Helmbold (Cambridge, MA, and London, 1957), p. 555.

22 Paquet, ed., *Les cyniques grecs*, p. 94. Also see the masterful analysis of Marie-Odile Goulet-Caze, *L'ascèse*

cynique: un commentaire de Diogène Laërce VI 70–71 (Paris, 1986).

23 Sophocles, *Antigone*, in *The Theban Plays of Sophocles*, trans. David R. Slavitt (New Haven, CT, and London, 2007), p. 3.

24 *The Works of Lucian*, pp. 179–81.

25 Diogenes, *Lives*, p. 67.

2 ROUSSEAU; OR, THE MILKY WAY

1 Jean-Jacques Rousseau, *Discourse on the Sciences and the Arts*, in *The Collected Writings of Rousseau*, vol. I, ed. Roger D. Masters and Christopher Kelly, trans. Judith R. Bush, Masters and Kelly (Hanover, NH, and London, 1992), pp. 20, 20 n.

2 Rousseau, 'Final Reply', in *The Collected Writings of Rousseau*, vol. I, p. 111.

3 Rousseau, *Discourse on the Sciences and the Arts*, p. 33, and 'Final Reply', p. 126.

4 Rousseau, 'Final Reply', p. 113.

5 Ibid., p. 117.

6 Rousseau, *Discourse on the Sciences and the Arts*, p. 12.

7 Rousseau, 'Final Reply', p. 116.

8 Ibid., p. 128.

9 Rousseau, *Discourse on the Origin, and Foundations of Inequality Among Men*, in *The Major Political Writings of Jean-Jacques Rousseau*, ed. and trans. John T. Scott (Chicago and London, 2012), p. 91.

10 Ibid., p. 65.

11 Ibid., p. 92.

12 Ibid.

13 Jean-Jacques Rousseau, *Emile; or, On Education*, trans. Allan Bloom (New York, 1979), p. 152.

14 Ibid., p. 191.

15 Ibid., pp. 191–2.

16 Ibid.

17 Voltaire, *Voltaire's Correspondence*, ed. and trans. Theodore Besterman (Geneva, 1953–65).

18 Rousseau, *Emile*, p. 352.

19 Ibid.

20 Jean-Jacques Rousseau, *Confessions*, trans. J. M. Cohen (Harmondsworth, 1953), p. 76.

21 Ibid.

22 Jean-Jacques Rousseau, *Julie; or, The New Heloïse*, trans. and ed. Phillip Stewart and Jean Vaché (Hanover, NH, 1997), pp. 372–3.

23 Rousseau, *Confessions*, p. 381.

24 Ibid.

25 Rousseau, *Emile*, p. 57.

26 Ibid., pp. 57–8.

27 Ibid., p. 58.

28 Rousseau, *Julie*, p. 372.

29 Ibid.

30 Ibid., p. 373.

31 Rousseau, *Emile*, p. 151.

32 Ibid.

33 Ibid., p. 153.

34 Ibid.

35 Ibid.

36 Ibid.

37 Rousseau, *Discourse on the Origin . . . of Inequality*, p. 124.

38 Jean-Jacques Rousseau, 'Essay on the Origin of Language', in *On the Origin of Languages: Two Essays*, trans. John H. Moran and Alexander Gode (Chicago and London, 1966), p. 41.

39 Ibid.

40 Rousseau, *Emile*, p. 346.

41 Louis-Antoine de Saint-Just, *Fragments d'institutions républicaines* (Paris, 1976), p. 264.

42 Joachim Fest, *Hitler*, trans. Richard Winston and Clara Winston (San Diego, New York and London, 1973), p. 535.

3 KANT; OR, ETHICAL ALCOHOLISM

1 Arsénij Goulyga, *Emmanuel Kant: une vie* (Paris, 1985), pp. 64–5.

2 Ehrgott André Charles Wasianski, 'Emmanuel Kant dans ses dernières années', in *Kant intime*, ed. Jean Mistler (Paris, 1985), p. 121.

3 Louis Ernst Borowski, 'Description de la vie et du caractère d'Emmanuel Kant', in *Kant intime*, ed. Mistler, p. 17.

4 Immanuel Kant, *Anthropology from a Pragmatic Point of View* [1798], trans. and ed. Robert B. Louden (Cambridge, 2006), p. 46.

5 Ibid.

6 Ibid., p. 49.

7 Ibid., p. 51.

8 Ibid., p. 50.

9 Ibid., p. 136.

10 Goulyga, *Emmanuel Kant*, p. 174.

11 Wasianski, 'Emmanuel Kant', p. 128.

12 Borowski, 'Description', p. 16.

13 Kant, *Anthropology*, p. 58.

14 Ibid., p. 62.

15 Ibid., pp. 62–3.

16 Ibid., p. 63.

17 Ibid.

18 Ibid.

19 Ibid.

20 Ibid., p. 64.

21 Kant, *Metaphysics of Morals*, trans. Mary Gregor (Cambridge, 1991), pp. 222–3.

22 Ibid., p. 223.

23 Ibid.

24 Ibid., pp. 223–4.

25 Reinhold Bernhard Jachmann, 'Emmanuel Kant dans des lettres à un ami', in *Kant intime*, ed. Mistler, p. 45.

26 Ibid., p. 47.

27 Wasianski, 'Emmanuel Kant', p. 74.

28 Jachmann, 'Emmanuel Kant', p. 51.

29 Ibid., p. 52.

30 Ibid., p. 45.

31 Immanuel Kant, *The Conflict of the Faculties* [1798], trans. Mary J. Gregor (New York 1979), p. 189.

32 Immanuel Kant, 'Essay on the Maladies of the Head' [1764], p. 72, *Cambridge books online*, http://ebooks. cambridge.org, accessed June 2012.

33 Immanuel Kant, 'Observations on the Feeling of the Beautiful and Sublime', p. 34, *Cambridge books online*, http://ebooks.cambridge.org, accessed June 2012.

34 Kant, 'Essay on the Maladies of the Head', p. 76.

35 Kant, *The Conflict of the Faculties,* p. 197.

36 Ibid.

37 Ibid, p. 209.

38 Borowski, 'Description', p. 15.

39 Kant, *The Conflict of the Faculties*, p. 209.

40 Wasianski, 'Emmanuel Kant', p. 149.

4 FOURIER; OR, THE PIVOTAL LITTLE PIE

1 Charles Fourier, *The Theory of the Four Movements*, ed. Gareth Stedman Jones, trans. Ian Patterson (Cambridge and New York, 1996), p. 178.

2 Charles Fourier, *La fausse industrie*, vol. VIII of *Oeuvres complètes* [OC], ed. Simone Debout (Paris, 1966–8), p. 442.

3 Ibid.

4 Fourier, *Le nouveau monde amoureux*, OC, vol. VII, pp. 257, 326.

5 Fourier, *Théorie de l'unité universelle*, OC, vol. V, p. 165.

6 Ibid., vol. II, p. 28.

7 Fourier, *Le nouveau monde amoureux*, OC, vol. VII, p. 138.

8 Fourier, *Théorie de l'unité universelle*, OC, vol. V, p. 418.

9 Ibid.

10 Ibid., p. 419.

11 Fourier, *Theory of the Four Movements*, p. 166.

12 Fourier, *Théorie de l'unité universelle*, OC, vol. V, p. 420.

13 Fourier, *Le nouveau monde amoureux*, OC, vol. VII, p. 136.

14 Fourier, *Théorie de l'unité universelle*, OC, vol. V, p. 420.

15 Fourier, *Le nouveau monde amoureux*, OC, vol. VII, p. 18.

16 Fourier, *Theory of the Four Movements*, p. 166.

17 Ibid. and *Théorie de l'unité universelle*, OC, vol. IV, p. 19.

18 Fourier, *Le nouveau monde industriel et sociétaire*, OC, vol. VI, p. 224.

19 Fourier, *Le nouveau monde amoureux*, OC, vol. VII, p. 20.

20 Ibid., p. 132.

21 Ibid., p. 131.

22 Fourier, *Le nouveau monde industriel et sociétaire*, OC, vol. VI, p. 253.

23 Ibid., p. 259.

24 Fourier, *Le nouveau monde amoureux*, OC, vol. VII, p. 19.

25 Ibid., p. 139.

26 Ibid., p. 140.

27 Ibid., p. 142.

28 Fourier, *Théorie de l'unité universelle*, OC, vol. V, p. 358.

29 Fourier, *Le nouveau monde industriel et sociétaire*, OC,
    vol. VI, p. 255.
30 Ibid., p. 256.
31 Ibid.
32 Fourier, *Le nouveau monde amoureux*, OC, vol. VII,
    p. 339.
33 Ibid., p. 339.
34 Ibid., p. 341.
35 Ibid., p. 343.
36 Ibid., p. 346.
37 Ibid., p. 356.
38 Fourier, *Théorie de l'unité universelle*, OC, vol. V, p. 358.
39 Fourier, *Le nouveau monde amoureux*, OC, vol. VII,
    p. 347.
40 Ibid., p. 357.
41 Ibid., p. 133.
42 Ibid., p. 113.
43 Fourier, *Theory of the Four Movements*, p. 168.
44 Ibid., p. 169.
45 Fourier, *Le nouveau monde amoureux*, OC, vol. VII, p. 135.
46 Ibid., p. 129.
47 Fourier, *Le nouveau monde industriel et sociétaire*, OC,
    vol. VI, p. 260.
48 Ibid.
49 Fourier, *Théorie de l'unité universelle*, OC, vol. IV, p. 243.
50 Ibid., p. 244.
51 Roland Barthes, *Sade, Fourier, Loyola*, trans. Richard
    Miller (Berkeley, CA, 1989), p. 99.

5 NIETZSCHE; OR, THE SAUSAGES OF THE ANTI-CHRIST

1 Friedrich Nietzsche, *Ecce Homo*, trans. Walter Kaufmann
   (New York and Toronto, 1969), p. 256.
2 Ibid., p. 240.

3 Ibid., p. 237.

4 Friedrich Nietzsche, *The Gay Science*, trans. Walter
   Kaufmann (New York and Toronto, 1974), pp. 34–5.

5 Friedrich Nietzsche, *The Birth of Tragedy*, trans. Walter
   Kaufmann (New York and Toronto, 1967), p. 5.

6 Nietzsche, *Gay Science*, p. 81.

7 Ibid., pp. 81–2.

8 Friedrich Nietzsche, *Daybreak*, trans. R. J. Hollingdale
   (Cambridge, 1982), p. 122.

9 Friedrich Nietzsche, *Twilight of the Idols*, trans. Walter
   Kaufmann (Harmondsworth, 1968), p. 47.

10 Nietzsche, *Gay Science*, p. 122.

11 Ibid., p. 123.

12 Ibid., p. 104.

13 Nietzsche, *Ecce Homo*, p. 238.

14 Friedrich Nietzsche, *Twilight of the Idols*, p. 61.

15 Nietzsche, *Ecce Homo*, p. 238.

16 Friedrich Nietzsche, 'The Wanderer and His Shadow',
    in *Human All Too Human*, trans. R. J. Hollingdale
    (Cambridge, 1996), p. 334.

17 Nietzsche, *Gay Science*, p. 193.

18 Friedrich Nietzsche, *The Case of Wagner*, trans. Walter
    Kaufmann (New York and Toronto, 1967), p. 165 [trans-
    lation modified].

19 Friedrich Nietzsche, *Selected Letters of Friedrich
    Nietzsche*, ed. and trans. Christopher Middleton
    (Chicago, 1969), p. 59.

20 Curt Paul Janz, *Nietzsche: Biographie*, trans. Marc B. de
    Launay et al. (Paris, 1984), vol. I, p. 306.

21 Jean-Jacques Rousseau, *Emile; or, On Education*, trans.
    Allan Bloom (New York, 1979), p. 153.

22 Friedrich Nietzsche, *Beyond Good and Evil*, trans. R. J.
    Hollingdale (Harmondsworth, 1973), pp. 145–6.

23 Ibid., p. 180.

24 Nietzsche, *Ecce Homo*, p. 239.

25 Janz, *Nietzsche*, vol. III, p. 274.

26 Nietzsche, *Ecce Homo*, p. 239.

27 Ibid., p. 237.

28 Janz, *Nietzsche*, vol. II, p. 245.

29 Ibid., vol. III, p. 113.

30 Friedrich Nietzsche, letter to his mother, no. 722, 17 July 1886: www.nietzschesource.org (accessed 1 January 2014).

31 Nietzsche, letter to his mother, no. 885, 3 August 1887: www.nietzschesource.org (accessed 1 January 2014).

32 Nietzsche, letter to his mother, no. 1005, 20 March 1988, www.nietzschesource.org (accessed 1 January 2014).

33 Nietzsche, *Ecce Homo*, p. 262.

34 Ibid., p. 237.

35 Nietzsche, letter to his mother, no. 768, 9 November 1878, letter to his sister, no. 862: www.nietzschesource.org (accessed 1 January 2014).

36 Friedrich Nietzsche, 'Schopenhauer as Educator', in *Untimely Meditations*, trans. R. J. Hollingdale (Cambridge, 1997), p. 178.

37 Nietzsche, *Ecce Homo*, p. 259.

6 MARINETTI; OR, THE EXCITED PIG

1 Filippo Tommaso Marinetti, *The Futurist Cookbook*, trans. Suzanne Brill (London, 1989), p. 36.

2 Ibid.

3 Ibid., p. 37.

4 Ibid., p. 33.

5 Ibid., p. 32.

6 Ibid., p. 21.

7 Ibid.

8 Ibid., pp. 37–8.

9   Ibid., p. 38.

10   Friedrich Nietzsche, *The Birth of Tragedy*, trans. Walter Kaufmann (New York and Toronto, 1967), pp. 31–2.

11   Marinetti, *Futurist Cookbook*, p. 133.

12   Ibid., p. 40.

13   Ibid., p. 143.

14   Ibid., p. 144.

15   Ibid., p. 162.

16   Ibid., p. 145.

17   Ibid., p. 152.

18   Ibid., p. 146.

19   Ibid., p. 147.

20   Ibid., p. 173.

21   Ibid., p. 160.

22   Ibid., p. 110.

23   Ibid., p. 111.

7 SARTRE; OR, THE REVENGE OF THE CRUSTACEANS

1   Simone de Beauvoir, *Adieux: A Farewell to Sartre*, trans. Patrick O'Brian (London, 1984), p. 332.

2   Ibid.

3   Ibid., p. 333.

4   See the analyses of Suzanne Lilar, *A propos de Sartre et de l'amour* (Paris, 1967).

5   Jean-Paul Sartre, *War Diaries: Notebooks from a Phony War*, trans. Quintin Hoare (London, 1984), p. 149.

6   Ibid., p. 153.

7   Jean-Paul Sartre, *Being and Nothingness*, trans. Hazel E. Barnes (London, 1958), p. 613.

8   Ibid. (translation modified).

9   Ibid., p. 614.

10   Alice Schwarzer, *After the Second Sex*, trans. Marianne Howarth (New York, 1984), p. 108.

11 Simone de Beauvoir, *The Prime of Life*, trans. Peter Green
    (New York, 1982), p. 107.

12 Annie Cohen-Solal, *Sartre: A Life*, trans. Anna Cancogni
    (London, 1987), p. 139.

13 Ibid.

14 Sartre, *War Diaries*, p. 122.

15 Cohen-Solal, *Sartre*, p. 179.

16 Sartre, *Being and Nothingness*, Part 3, Chapter 2,
    pp. 306–39.

17 Ibid., p. 157.

18 Ibid. (translation modified).

19 Cohen-Solal, *Sartre*, p. 374 (translation modified).

20 Beauvoir, *Adieux*, p. 47.

21 Sartre, *Being and Nothingness*, p. 627.

22 Sartre, interview in *Actuel*, February 1973, no. 28.

23 Sartre, *Being and Nothingness*, pp. 596–7.

24 Jean-Paul Sartre, *The Psychology of the Imagination*
    (New York, 1948), p. 226.

25 Beauvoir, *The Prime of Life*, p. 169 (translation modified).

26 Ibid.

27 Jean-Paul Sartre, *Nausea*, trans. Robert Baldick (London,
    1963), p. 89.

28 Jean-Paul Sartre, *Words*, trans. Irene Clephane
    (Harmondsworth, 1967), pp. 96–7 (translation modified).

29 Jean-Paul Sartre, *The Condemned of Altona*, trans. Sylvia
    and George Leeson (New York, 1963), p. 65.

30 Sartre, *Being and Nothingness*, p. 615.

31 Beauvoir, *Adieux*, p. 333.

32 Ibid., p. 334.

33 Ibid.

34 Ibid., p. 409.

35 Cohen-Solal, *Sartre*, p. 373 (translation modified).

36 Beauvoir, *Adieux*, p. 332.

37 Sartre, *Being and Nothingness*, p. 615.

38 Beauvoir, *Adieux*, p. 230.
39 Sartre, *Nausea*, p. 116.
40 Sartre, *Being and Nothingness*, p. 599 (translation modified).
41 Ibid., p. 604.
42 Ibid., p. 614.
43 Sartre, *Words*, p. 84.
44 Sartre, *Nausea*, p. 144.
45 Ibid., p. 178.

CONCLUSION: THE GAY SCIENCE OF EATING

1 Annick le Guerer, 'The Philosophical Nose', in *Scents*, trans. Richard Miller (London, 1993).
2 Gilles Deleuze and Félix Guattari, *Anti-Oedipus*, trans. Robert Hurley, Mark Seem and Helen R. Lane (Minneapolis, MN, 1983), and *A Thousand Plateaus*, trans. Brian Massumi (Minneapolis, MN, 1987).
3 Jacques Lacarrière, *The Gnostics*, trans. Nina Rootes (London, 1977).
4 René Major, 'La logique du nom proper et le transfert', *Confrontation*, no. 15 (Paris, 1986), pp. 147–64; *La discernement* (Paris, 1984); and *De l'élection* (Paris, 1992).
5 Auguste Hamon, SJ, *Sainte Marguerite-Marie* (Paris, 1922), p. 90.
6 Ibid., p. 242. Cf. Colette Yver, *Marguerite-Marie, messagère du Christ* (Paris, 1937).
7 Ibid., p. 89.
8 Ibid., p. 20.
9 Donatien-Alphonse-François de Sade, *Juliette*, trans. Austryn Wainhouse (New York, 1968), p. 421.
10 Noëlle Châtelet, 'Le libertin au table', in *Sade: écrire la crise. Actes du colloque de Cerisy*, ed. Philippe Roger and Michel Camus (Paris, 1983).

11 Donatien-Alphonse-François de Sade, *Oeuvres complètes*, vol. IV (Paris, 1961), p. 198.

12 Sade, *Juliette*, p. 1187; Châtelet, 'Le libertin au table', p. 81.

13 Donatien-Alphonse-François de Sade, *Justine; or, The Misfortunes of Virtue*, trans. John Phillips (Oxford, 2012), p. 136.

14 Cited by Béatrice Fink, 'Lecture alimentaire de l'utopie sadienne', in *Sade: écrire la crise*, p. 175.

15 For the Russian incident, see Simone de Beauvoir, *Force of Circumstance*, trans. Richard Howard (London, 1965), p. 307; for the Japanese one, *Adieux: A Farewell to Sartre*, trans. Patrick O'Brian (London, 1984), p. 331; and for the Moroccan one, *The Prime of Life*, trans. Peter Green (New York, 1962), p. 263.

Bibliography

Aron, Jean-Paul, *Le mangeur du xixe siècle* (Paris, 1976)

Badinter, Elisabeth, and Robert Badinter, *Condorcet* (Paris, 1989)

Baillet, Adrien, *La vie de Monsieur Descartes* (Paris, 2012)

Barthes, Roland, *Sade, Fourier, Loyola*, trans. Richard Miller (Berkeley, CA, 1989)

Beauvoir, Simone de, *Adieux: A Farewell to Sartre*, trans. Patrick O'Brian (London, 1984)

—, *Force of Circumstance*, trans. Richard Howard (London, 1965)

—, *The Prime of Life*, trans. Peter Green (New York, 1982)

Borowski, Louis Enst, 'Description de la vie et du caractère d'Emmanuel Kant', in *Kant intime*, ed. Jean Mistler (Paris, 1985)

Brillat-Savarin, J. A., *The Physiology of Taste*, trans. M.F.K. Fisher (New York and London, 2009)

Castelot, André, *L'histoire à table* (Paris, 1979)

Châtelet, Noëlle, *Le corps à corps culinaire* (Paris, 1998)

—, 'Le libertin au table', in *Sade: écrire la crise. Actes du colloque de Cerisy*, ed. Philippe Roger and Michel Camus (Paris, 1983)

Chrysostom, Dio, 'The Sixth Discourse: Diogenes; or, On Tyranny', in *Discourses 1–11*, trans. J. W. Colhoon (Cambridge, MA, 1932)

Clastres, Pierre, *Chronicle of the Guayaki Indians*, trans. Paul Auster (New York, 1998)

Cohen-Solal, Annie, *Sartre: A Life*, trans. Anna Cancogni (London, 1987)

Colerus, Jean, 'The Life of B. de Spinoza', in *Spinoza: His Life and Philosophy*, trans. Frederick Pollock (London, 1880)

Davidenko, Dimitri, *Descartes le scandaleux* (Paris, 1988)

Deleuze, Gilles, and Félix Guattari, *Anti-Oedipus*, trans. Robert Hurley, Mark Seem and Helen R. Lane (Minneapolis, MN, 1983)

—, *A Thousand Plateaus*, trans. Brian Massumi (Minneapolis, MN, 1987)

Detienne, Marcel, 'Culinary Practices and the Spirit of Sacrifice', in *The Cuisine of Sacrifice Among the Greeks*, ed. Marcel Detienne and Jean-Paul Vernant, trans. Paula Wissing (Chicago and London, 1989)

—, *Dionysos Slain*, trans. Mireille Muellner and Leonard Muellner (Baltimore, MD, and London, 1979)

Didier, Raymond, *Schopenhauer* (Paris, 1997)

Fest, Joachim, *Hitler*, trans. Richard Winston and Clara Winston (San Diego, New York and London, 1973)

Feuerbach, Ludwig, *Manifestes philosophiques: textes choisis, 1839–1845*, trans. Louis Althusser (Paris, 1960)

—, *Pensées diverses* (Paris, 1987)

Fink, Béatrice, 'Lecture alimentaire de l'utopie sadienne', in *Sade: écrire la crise. Actes du colloque de Cerisy*, ed. Philippe Roger and Michel Camus (Paris, 1983)

Flem, Lydia, *La vie quotidienne de Freud et de ses patients* (Paris, 1986)

Foucault, Michel, *The Use of Pleasure* (London, 1991)

Fourier, Charles, *Oeuvres complètes*, II–V: *Théorie de l'unité universelle*, ed. Simone Debout (Paris, 1966–8)

—, *Oeuvres complètes*, VI: *Le nouveau monde industriel et sociétaire*, ed. Simone Debout (Paris, 1966–8)

—, *Oeuvres complètes*, VII: *Le nouveau monde amoureux*, ed. Simone Debout (Paris, 1966–8)

—, *Oeuvres complètes*, VIII: *La fausse industrie*, ed. Simone
   Debout (Paris, 1966–8)

—, *The Theory of the Four Movements*, ed. Gareth Fourier
   Stedman Jones, trans. Ian Patterson (Cambridge and
   New York, 1996)

Goulet-Caze, Marie-Odile, *L'Ascèse cynique: Un commentaire
   de Diogène Laërce VI 70–71* (Paris, 1986)

Goulyga, Arsénij, *Emmanuel Kant: une vie* (Paris, 1985)

Guerer, Annick le, 'The Philosophical Nose', in *Scents*,
   trans. Richard Miller (London, 1993)

Hamon, Auguste, SJ, *Sainte Marguerite-Marie*
   (Paris, 1922)

Hegel, G.W.F., *Briefe von und an Hegel*, ed. Joseph Hoffmeister
   (Hamburg, 1952)

—, *Lectures on the Philosophy of History*, trans. E. S. Haldane
   (London, 1892)

Jachmann, Reinhold Bernhard, 'Emmanuel Kant dans
   des lettres à un ami', in *Kant intime*, ed. Jean Mistler
   (Paris, 1985)

Janz, Curt Paul, *Nietzsche: biographie*, trans. Marc B. de
   Launay et al. (Paris, 1984)

Kant, Immanuel, *Anthropology from a Pragmatic Point
   of View* [1798], trans. and ed. Robert B. Louden
   (Cambridge, 2006)

—, *The Conflict of the Faculties* [1798], trans. Mary J. Gregor
   (New York, 1979)

—, 'Essay on the Maladies of the Head' [1764], p. 72,
   Cambridge books online: http://ebooks.cambridge.org,
   accessed June 2012

—, *The Metaphysics of Morals*, trans. Mary Gregor
   (Cambridge, 1991)

—, 'Observations on the Feeling of the Beautiful and
   Sublime', *Cambridge books online*: http://ebooks.cambridge
   .org, accessed June 2012

La Mettrie, Julien Offray de, *L'art de jouir* (Potsdam, 1751)

—, *Man a Machine* [1748], in *Man a Machine & Man a Plant*, trans. Richard A Watson and Maya Rybalka (Indianapolis, IN, and Cambridge, MA, 1994)

Lacarrière, Jacques, *The Gnostics*, trans. Nina Rootes (London, 1977)

Laërtius, Diogenes, 'Lettre à Monime', in *Les cyniques grecs*, ed. Léonce Paquet (Ottawa, 1988)

—, *Lives of the Eminent Philosophers*, trans. R. D. Hicks (London and New York, 1925)

Lévi-Strauss, Claude, *Tristes tropiques,* trans. John Russell (New York, 1971)

Lilar, Suzanne, *A propos de Sartre et de l'amour* (Paris, 1967)

Lucian, *The Works of Lucian of Samosata*, trans. H. W. Fowler and F. G. Fowler, vol. IV (Oxford, 1905)

Major, René, *De l'election* (Paris, 1992)

—, *La discernement* (Paris, 1984)

—, 'La logique du nom proper et le transfert', *Confrontation*, 15 (Paris, 1986)

Marinetti, Filippo Tommaso, *The Futurist Cookbook*, trans. Suzanne Brill (London, 1989)

Montaigne, Michel de, *Essays*, trans. and ed. M. A. Screech (London, 1991)

Nietzsche, Friedrich, *Beyond Good and Evil*, trans. R. J. Hollingdale (Harmondsworth, 1973)

—, *The Birth of Tragedy*, trans. Walter Kaufmann (New York and Toronto, 1967)

—, *The Case of Wagner*, trans. Walter Kaufmann (New York and Toronto, 1967)

—, *Daybreak*, trans. R. J. Hollingdale (Cambridge, 1982)

—, *Ecce Homo*, trans. Walter Kaufmann (New York and Toronto, 1969)

—, *The Gay Science*, trans. Walter Kaufmann (New York and Toronto, 1974)

——, letter to his mother, no. 722, 17 July 1886: www.nietzschesource.org (accessed 1 January 2014)

——, letter to his mother, no. 768, 9 November 1878: www.nietzschesource.org (accessed 1 January 2014)

——, letter to his mother, no. 885, 3 August 1887: www.nietzschesource.org (accessed 1 January 2014)

——, letter to his mother, no. 1005, 20 March 1888: www.nietzschesource.org (accessed 1 January 2014)

——, letter to his sister, no. 862: www.nietzschesource.org (accessed 1 January 2014)

——, 'Schopenhauer as Educator', in *Untimely Meditations*, trans. R. J. Hollingdale (Cambridge, 1997)

——, *Selected Letters of Friedrich Nietzsche*, ed. and trans. Christopher Middleton (Chicago, 1969)

——, *Twilight of the Idols*, trans. Walter Kaufmann (Harmondsworth, 1968)

——, 'The Wanderer and His Shadow', in *Human All Too Human*, trans. R. J. Hollingdale (Cambridge, 1996)

Plato, *The Republic*, trans. Robin Waterfield (Oxford, 1993)

Plutarch, 'De esu carnium I', in *Plutarch's Moralia*, vol. XII, trans. Harold Cherniss and William C. Helmbold (Cambridge, MA, and London, 1957)

Revel, Jean-François, *Un festin en paroles* (Paris, 1982)

Rousseau, Jean-Jacques, *Confessions*, trans. J. M. Cohen (Harmondsworth, 1953)

——, *Discourse on the Origin, and Foundations of Inequality Among Men*, in *The Major Political Writings of Jean-Jacques Rousseau*, ed. and trans. John T. Scott (Chicago and London, 2012)

——, *Discourse on the Sciences and the Arts*, in *The Collected Writings of Rousseau*, vol. I, ed. Roger D. Masters and Christopher Kelly, trans. Judith R. Bush, Masters and Kelly (Hanover, NH, and London, 1992)

—, *Emile; or, On Education*, trans. Allan Bloom
  (New York, 1979)
—, 'Essay on the Origin of Language', in *On the Origin of
  Languages: Two Essays*, trans. John H. Moran and
  Alexander Gode (Chicago and London, 1966)
—, 'Final Reply', in *The Collected Writings of Rousseau*,
  vol. I, ed. Roger D. Masters and Christopher Kelly, trans.
  Judith R. Bush, Roger D. Masters and Christopher Kelly
  (Hanover, NH, and London, 1992)
—, *Julie; or, The New Heloïse*, trans. and ed. Phillip Stewart
  and Jean Vaché (Hanover, NH, 1997)
Sade, Donatien-Alphonse-François de, *Juliette*, trans. Austryn
  Wainhouse (New York, 1968)
—, *Justine; or, The Misfortunes of Virtue*, trans. John Phillips
  (Oxford, 2012)
—, *Oeuvres complètes*, vol. IV (Paris, 1961)
Saint-Just, Louis-Antoine de, *Fragments d'institutions
  républicaines* (Paris, 1976)
Sartre, Jean-Paul, interview in *Actuel*, no. 28 (February 1973)
—, *Being and Nothingness*, trans. Hazel E. Barnes
  (London, 1958)
—, *The Condemned of Altona*, trans. Sylvia Leeson and
  George Leeson (New York, 1963)
—, *Nausea*, trans. Robert Baldick (London, 1963)
—, *The Psychology of Imagination* (New York, 1948)
—, *War Diaries: Notebooks from a Phony War*, trans.
  Quintin Hoare (London, 1984)
—, *Words*, trans. Irene Clephane (Harmondsworth, 1967)
Schwarzer, Alice, *After the Second Sex*, trans. Marianne
  Howarth (New York, 1984)
Serres, Michel, *The Five Senses*, trans. Margaret Sankey
  and Peter Crowley (London and New York, 2008)
Sophocles, *Antigone*, in *The Theban Plays of Sophocles*, trans.
  David R. Slavitt (New Haven, CT, and London, 2007)

Vernant, Jean-Paul, 'At Man's Table', in *The Cuisine of Sacrifice Among the Greeks*, ed. Marcel Detienne and Jean-Paul Vernant, trans. Paula Wissing (Chicago and London, 1989)

Voltaire, *Voltaire's Correspondence*, ed. and trans. Theodore Besterman (Geneva, 1953–65)

Wasianski, E.A.C., 'Emmanuel Kant dans ses dernières années', in *Kant intime*, ed. Jean Mistler (Paris, 1985)

Yver, Colette, *Marguerite-Marie, messagère du Christ* (Paris, 1937)